“The Pacific Ocean, Gulf of Alaska
are unforgiving and harsh environn
and survive all four with the nerve and skill that Jerry wielded.”

Craig Cross
Aleutian Spray Fisheries

“My first job out of college was on a ship anchored in Dutch Harbor, Alaska. I worked as a foreman for Jerry processing King crab. My initiation, putting in twelve hours a day seven days a week for six months until we cooked, froze, and packed what seemed like every dang crab in the universe. (Kinda like this COVID-19 virus thing: we worked, we went nowhere, we slept, we went back to work.) Jerry made this life all seem normal.

As a kid, I got up at 5:00 a.m. and delivered newspapers in downtown Bremerton, Washington. When Jerry was a kid, he got up at 4:00 a.m. and started up his Dad’s Dungeness crab cannery in Westport, Washington. If everyone worked as hard as Jerry, the world would be well fed, and the word obese would fade from our vocabulary.

We all get to do cool, interesting stuff on occasion; Jerry just did it all the time most every day, as you will read. Jerry is no John Steinbeck, but other than his trip to the Sea of Cortez in Mexico Steinbeck never came close to having as many adventures and close scrapes as Jerry. I’m very proud he didn’t wear me out. My wife does that now.”

Dan Hallman
Superintendent at former SeaWest Industries

“It would be difficult to write an endorsement for Jerry’s book in just a sentence or two. In fact if I were to write a book about my life, Jerry would be in most of the chapters.

Jerry is the real deal. He is like the Indiana Jones of the seafood industry. When the “Dos Equis Man” announced his retirement, I told Jerry there was a job opening for the most interesting man in the world, and he should apply.

The stories of Jerry’s exploits will amaze most people. Jerry has had an adventure-packed life.”

Steve Martin
Case Marine & Industrial

“Jerry has a unique ability to convey his startling, sometimes terrifying experiences of fishing in Alaska with a combination of vividness, humor, and warmth. We had plenty of adventures traveling to Russia together and the Russians loved him.”

Tony Allison
Former CEO of Marine Resources Company International

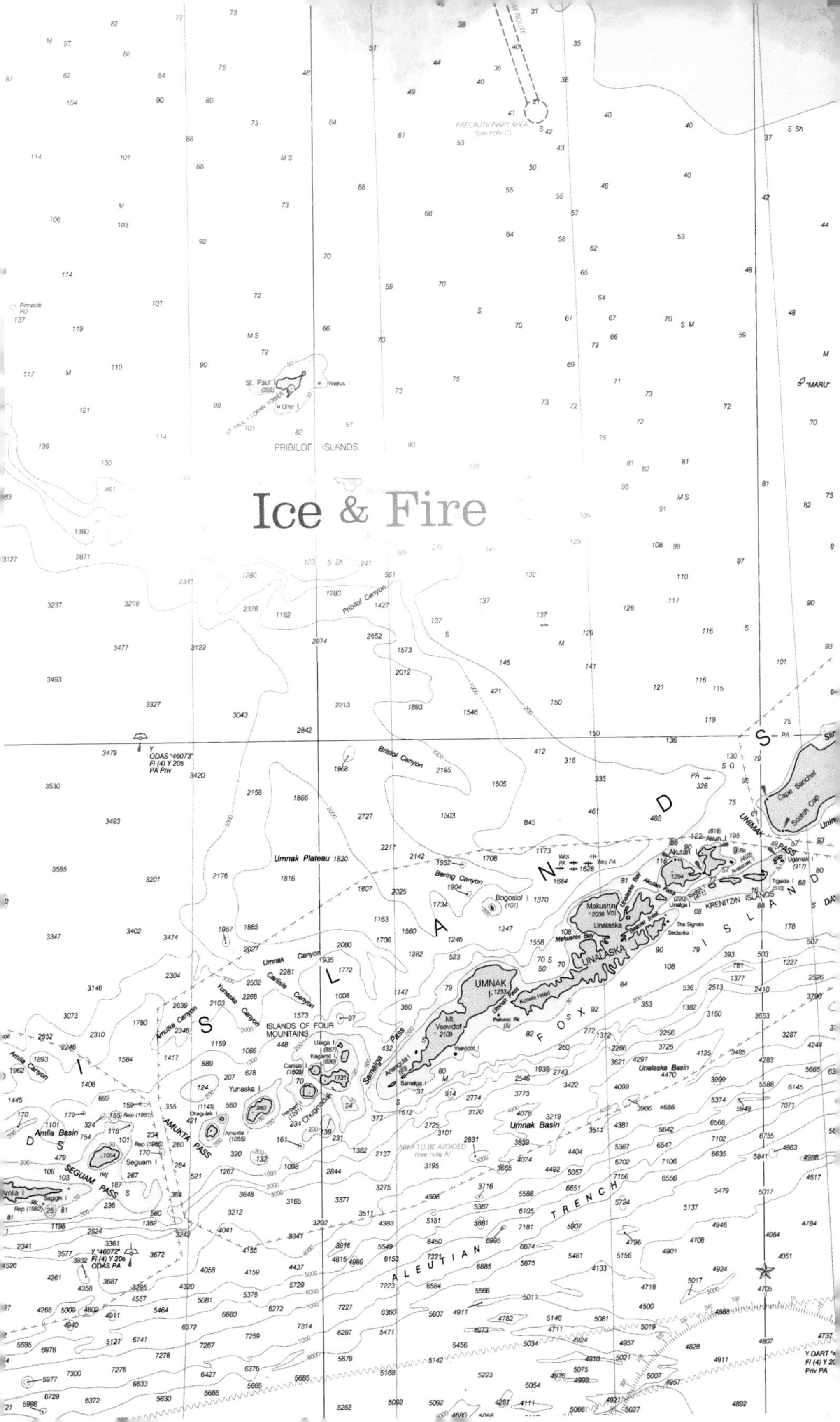
Ice & Fire
PRECAUTIONARY AREA (see note C)
St. Paul I
Walrus I
Otter I
ST PAUL I LORAN TOWER
PRIBILOF ISLANDS
"MARU"
Pribilof Canyon
Bristol Canyon
Umnak Plateau
Bering Canyon
Bogoslof I
Y ODAS "46073" Fl (4) Y 20s PA Priv
Umnak Canyon
Carlisle Canyon
Yunaska Canyon
Amukta Canyon
Amlia Canyon
ISLANDS OF FOUR MOUNTAINS
Samalga Pass
UMNAK I.
Mt. Vsevidof
UNALASKA
Makushin Vol
Unalaska
Akutan I
Akun I
KRENITZIN ISLANDS
UNIMAK PASS
Cape Sarichef
Scotch Cap
Umnak Basin
Unalaska Basin
Amlia Basin
SEGUAM PASS
AMUKTA PASS
Seguam I
Yunaska I
Amlia I
AREA TO BE AVOIDED (see note A)
ALEUTIAN TRENCH
FOX ISLANDS
Y "46072" Fl (4) Y 20s ODAS PA
Y DART Fl (4) Y 20 Priv PA

Ice & Fire

The Powerful and Frightening Adventures of Survival in Alaska and the Aleutian Islands

by Captain Jerry Tilley, Sr.

WHALER
JET
PRESS

Ice & Fire: The Powerful and Frightening Adventures of Survival in Alaska and the Aleutian Islands

Copyright © 2020 Jerry Tilley Sr.
All rights reserved. No part of this book may be reproduced or transmitted in any form or by any means, electronic or mechanical including photocopying, recording or by any information retrieval system, without written permission of Jerry Tilley Sr.

For Information
Whaler Press
P.O. Box 2453
Lynnwood, WA 98036
WhalerPress@gmail.com
www.facebook.com/WhalerPress/
www.novafish.com

Contributions made by SunWave Properties, L.L.C.

Book design by Michael Brady Design
Publishing Coach by Trudy B. Catterfeld, BookMarketingNext
Front cover and back cover design by Anita Jones, Anotherjonesgraphics
Edited by K.D. Kragen, KaveDragen Inc L.L.C.

Some names and identifying details have been changed to protect the privacy of individuals.

Published 2020

ISBN-13: 978-17350081-0-3
Library of Congress Control Number: 2020908799
Whaler Press, Lynnwood, Washington

Photo credits: Courtesy of the author, viii, x, xiii, xiv, xiv, xv, xv, xvi, xvi, 1, 22, 23, 24, 25, 26, 54, 62, 88, 94, 95, 100, 139, 140, 142, 144, 147, 155, 156, 157, 157, 157, 157, 157, 157, 158, 158, 159, 159; courtesy Robert Simon, ix, 160; National Oceanographic and Atmospheric Administration, i, ii–iii, vi, xxii, 102, 138, 158; United States Navy, 63; Emiliano Arano, Pexels, xx–xxi, 137; Associated Press, 70; Vladimir Bezugliy, Shutterstock, 18; Stephen Barnes/Transport, Alamy Stock Photo, 108; Blaque X, Pexels, 17; Camila Castillo, Unsplash, 83; Torsten Dederichs, Unsplash, 40; Guillaume Groult, Unsplash, 74; Matt Hardy, Unsplash, 55; Viktor Jakovlev, Unsplash, 8; Justin Judd, 129; Tim Marshall, Unsplash, iv–v; Mockup Graphics, Unsplash, 48; NaluPhoto. iStock, 113; Jason Rojas, Unsplash, 30; Alexandra Rose, Unsplash, 155; Enrico Smeraldi, Pexels, 117; Ivan Suprunov, Shutterstock, 93; stockphoto-graf, Shutterstock, 89; Jamie Street, Unsplash, 38; uk.boats.com, 45; Vlad Tchompalov, Unsplash, 33; Will Terra, Unsplash, 90; TMON, Shutterstock, 149; welcomia, Shutterstock, 36; Ben Wiid, Unsplash, xviii; Ashley Wiley, iStock, 14; ymphotos, Shutterstock, 124;

Dedication

How deep and intense does the friendship go?
There are no measurements, so I don't know
An admiration I have always had that lasts
Remembering times that we had a blast
Not forgotten that aggressive selling machine
A personal driving force seldom seen
Above the status quo, we would be climbin'
Inspired, this book I dedicate to Bob Simon

Contents

Foreword

I met Jerry Tilley ("Jet") in the fall of 1980 when he and his wonderful business partners hired me to join SeaWest Industries, a remarkable business venture they pioneered in Alaska fisheries. SeaWest shaped the future of fisheries into the 21st century. Jet also shaped my own company, which began in 1986, and has operated continuously since.

Each morning in the predawn hours, Jet and I would show up for work well before others. He would often be at a drafting table working on the blueprint for the design of a piece of equipment or a processing line or for the conversion of a ship. As much work as there was to be done before the sun came up and others arrived at work, Jet would occasionally take a moment to share with me some of his experiences and wisdom. As the years went on, I would hear from many others about their own memories of Jet's contributions and accomplishments. As my own business achieved success, I came to realize that the benefits I had gained from my time with Jet should be shared. Those years with Jet were for me an outlier opportunity. I was in the right place at the right time to hear about and learn and benefit—first hand—from this man's work and contributions.

Today, decades later, with over 90 percent of the seafood that is consumed in the United States coming from countries other than our own United States waters, Jet is recognized as a globetrotting seafood industry pioneer. He educated fishers and processors on how to technically, fiscally, and responsibly advance one fishery after another. From fisheries in Alaska, across the Pacific Ocean to Russia, south into Asian fishing ventures, still farther south into

South America, and around the Cape up into the North Atlantic fisheries, Jet's reach has shaped fisheries worldwide. How can this be? Imagine what a restaurant menu or grocery display might look like if the seafood were only that which came directly from a hook or out of a net or trap.

What Jet pioneered was how to bring the commodity of the catch, through innovative manufacturing practices and understanding of the market, to the finished, convenient, consistent forms we as restaurant goers and grocery shoppers take for granted.

The seafood industry is diverse, with the catch coming from over one hundred countries, representing hundreds of species, and many more product forms. Add to this reality: when the catch is pulled on board, there are often literally hundreds of thousands of pounds, fished in just hours. Jerry Tilley is a pioneer whose creative contributions have harnessed this diversity and produced convenience from the abundance.

Jet's stories are about a remarkable American who advanced fisheries practices around the world. You will see from his writing he is also a Renaissance Man. While on forays around the world, so often isolated and distant for long periods, Jet wrote—and now shares—inspired stories and poems. In this volume you have a literary and historical legacy that stands beside Jerry Tilley's business and technological innovations.

Robert Simon
CEO, NOVA Fisheries, Inc.

www.novafish.com

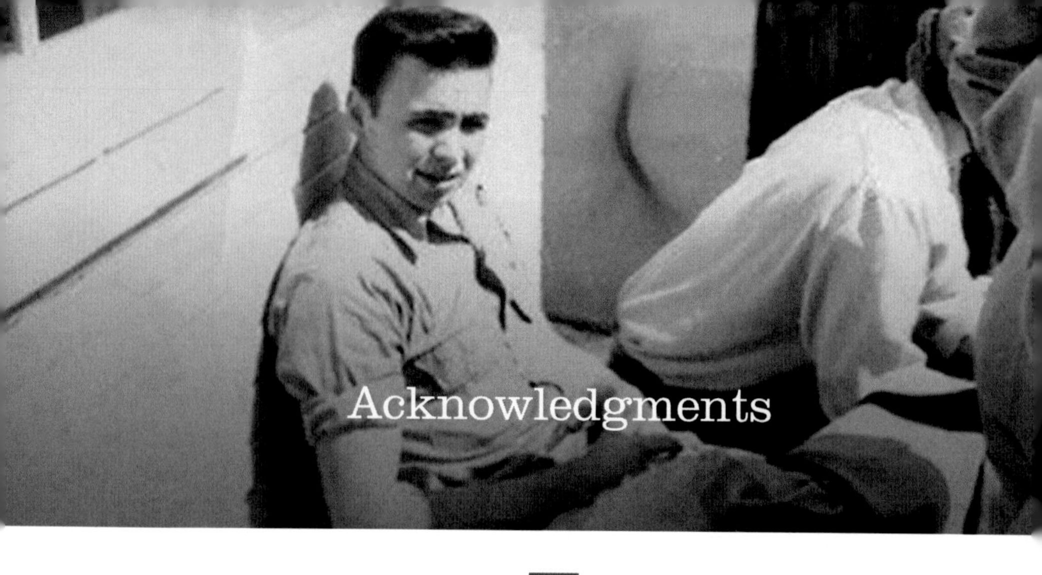

Acknowledgments

This book was written as a history of what I did from birth to the present day for the benefit of my children, grandchildren, great-grandchildren, and great-great-grandchildren. As I was growing up, I never knew what my grandfather Tilley's given name was. I only knew my grandfather on my mother's side. I never knew what they did or where they came from. I didn't want my offspring to wonder and find it necessary to ask anyone, "What did Grampa do?"

With that said, I must give thanks to many who have made a difference in my life. The one person who allowed this book to be published, the one who was convinced it required printing and helped get the process going is Bob Simon, a very dear friend and a well of kindness and a co-worker for many years. Thanks to Bob for introducing me to Trudy Catterfeld, my publisher and advisor. She possesses a wealth of knowledge in the procedures required to publish and hopefully get the book on the shelf. Michael Brady, for his unique creativity and technical skill in book design. Photographer Chelan Lenay, for the successful editorial assignments.

For those who got me started in life: my father Allen Douglas Tilley Sr. who was responsible for my work ethic and perfectionism to the point of great irritation to many. My mother, who insisted that I grow up with manners and clean, ironed clothes. My sister Lorene, who survived with me from the wrath of my mother's temper.

Donna Smith Tilley, my wife for 9 years and the mother of my

Above: Jerry Tilley Sr., age 18, at the cannery in Westport, Washington.

two daughters and one son. Joann Blake Tilley, my wife for 40 years. Cancer claimed her. Her daughter Jana, who joined my family at age 10. Joe and Sandy Pirak, for 56 years as close as families can get without being blood relatives. Bill and Zona Howell, so close like part of the family. Don and Sharon Tucker, our Dutch Harbor neighbor. Sharon, Joann's Dutch Harbor best friend and beyond to the end. Jim Severns, my diving partner and the toughest and strongest guy I have ever known. His wife Amiko, a better shipboard and landlubber cook would be almost impossible to find. Steve Martin, my chief engineer, best friend, and hunting partner for 30 years. Skip Greene, who started working for me in 1957 in Wrangell, Alaska, and followed me to Kodiak where we worked and shipped together for many years. The best man at my weddings and me at his weddings. A more stoic individual does not exist. RIP Skippy.

Peggy June Ostrom Schultz, my cousin. The one person responsible, who convinced me to put my life-threatening stories in writing. I did. All short stories in a loose-leaf binder. Then I started this book. Thank you, PJ.

For those who will be forever in my thoughts and have passed on to see the Pearly Gates. Jim Poor, the one man responsible for getting me to Alaska. Our friendship started in the 5th grade in Westport, Washington. Charlie Warner, my moose hunting partner for over 20 years. We always scored. Marion Parker, owner of Aleutian Divers in Kodiak. We dove together for 10 years. Died in a plane crash returning from a dive job.

Dick Pace, the man who hired me to help with the design of the equipment, supervise the installation, and take the liberty ship *Vita* to Dutch Harbor. Ray Martin, manager of Pacific Northern Airlines in Kodiak. This man saved my life by sending me to the hospital in Seattle to his doctor when I had spinal meningitis. Andy Bottlik, a master machinist unparalleled in his trade. Jimmy Gilman, a master at preparing and feeding great food to hundreds with the greatest of ease. My life-long friends Jack and Ruth Strong.

My utmost admiration for Darryl Pederson and Benny Binschus, my two partners in SeaWest Industries. Friends for life. Chuck Bundrant, a family friend for 55 years from Kodiak and beyond. Pete Hale from high school. A body full of North Korean shrapnel couldn't kill this Marine.

All the men and women who have made my life easier, successful, and complete in Alaska processing business: Craig Cross, Larry Dutton, Dan Hallman, Steve Borgerson, Don Tucker, Maurene MacDonald, Deblynne Whittlesy, Vala Hallgrimson, Trish Kaminsky, Chuck Petzel, Jim Mouser, Bob Woods, Andy Bottlik, Jim Severns, Bill Howell, Jon Dent, Kevin Thomson, Marty Hanna, Arne Jones, and Joe Pirak.

Great neighbors and closest of friends. I just must thank all of them for guidance and friendship. Mike and Sue Collins, for all the meals, assistance, and being there in time of need. Beau Finley, the artistic stone mason, a master at his trade. Then there are Arne and Nona Finley, my neighbors and security guards. If you drove into my driveway, Arne would be there wanting to know what, why, and who.

Facing page: On a barge in Westport, Washington, are Jerry Tilley, age 18; Jim Poor to the right on the porch; Ron Spoon, foreground, and his wife Irene Spoon, standing.

Introduction

The stories in this book are real experiences in my life with no embellishments.

Part I consists of outdoor adventures on land, in the air, on and under the sea. Part II tells about my thrill in intellectual challenges to innovate and design conversions of boats into thriving businesses which could process seafood out at sea instead of on shore.

Through the power of story, I venture to introduce you to the passion of a seaman and an inventor making novel and radical changes in the seafood industry.

Plunging into the sea, flying in dangerous weather, underwater detonations can be done successfully with calculated risk. However, sometimes the best laid plan can surprise and astonish you with unexpected disadvantages. I hope to bring to life how I could survive some of these hazardous adventures by trusting my instincts.

Catching crab and shrimp in the Gulf of Alaska and the Bering Sea is a highly perishable business. Those catcher boats depend on the nearby processing vessels waiting in bays close to the grounds to offload their catch, allowing them to return to the fishing grounds quickly. Successful onboard processing is a dangerous career and a complicated operation, but it is the key to success in the seafood business. This industry was an exciting wild territory for me. It lured my curiosity to explore and find uncharted solutions, creating new opportunities that made a difference for people and businesses.

These episodes are not in chronological order but go back and forth between scenes of adventure that resonate love, humor, rebound . . . and much gratification.

I was born in Tokeland, Washington, on August 25, 1931. Back in those days, you had to be tough just to survive. My mother had to be tough as well. My father was a fisherman, and he was also tough. No slack was given regardless of age. We had chores and didn't complain, because we just figger'd that was growing up. No huggin', no kissin', just get your job done. Do it exactly as you're told. Perfection will pass; anything less will not. If you are being pushed around by someone bigger than you, pick up an equalizer. "If you lose, don't come crying to me," my father would say.

In every school I attended I was the smallest for my age, and it was evident to me that I was never going to get any bigger. I had to show that I was stalwart and unyielding. It only worked on those my size. For the big boys, the use of the equalizer got me in trouble. However, it got me out of trouble by those who pursued brave ambitions.

I started working at age 5, peeling spuds with my brother in the kitchen of my dad's restaurant. No child labor laws back then.

Left: Jerry is demonstrating skills he learned in tap-dancing lessons with his dance partner in Cle Elum, Washington. 1936; right: Jerry's children, Dorothy Louise, Kathleen Ann, and "Corky" Jerry Jr., Westport, Washington, 1959.

I watched hogs getting butchered at a family farm where my school friend's family worked. My friend, who was 6, worked along with his older brother removing guts from the slaughtered hogs. It was the farm where my dad got his meat for the restaurant.

I turned out for football along with every other kid in school. The smallest pair of pants the school had for football players was too long, the knee pads were at my ankles. The big boys, thought it would be fun if they threw me over the goal post. They did. To them, it was funny; to me, it was a realization that fear would not be one of my attributes. I ran everywhere and could outrun just about all comers.

At 11, I started working for 65 cents an hour butchering Dungeness crab. My dad built a cannery, and I went to work there. At 14, I designed a machine that removed shells from the crab meat that had been shaken out by the workers. I also designed a new crab cannery for my dad's plant in Blaine, Washington. At 17, I supervised the cannery construction, and the contractor was skeptical until he saw my plans.

I watched a man putting all new tires on a logging truck across from where I was living. I walked over there and asked him if he

t: Jerry and dive partner Walter Nestell, 1962; right: Jerry and Wolf, 1965.

needed any help in his logging camp. "Can you drive a logging truck?" he asked. I replied, "No problem." I had never driven a truck that size, but I had driven my dad's big ice truck hauling ice from Aberdeen to Westport and a GMC cab-over flatbed. I drove that logging truck until that whole section was cleared.

I got married at 19. We had a daughter a year later. I went to work setting chokers in old-growth forest. Trees a thousand years old and older. An accident put three of us in the hospital. I had a broken back. I refused surgery. I wore a back brace with metal rods to hold me up. I was paralyzed from the hip down. That only lasted three months. Many trips to a chiropractor got me walking. Another daughter arrived while I was out of commission.

Off to Alaska, and I never turned back.

I was in Yakutat, Alaska, processing Dungeness crab when a radio call got my immediate attention. They said, "You have a son." Added, "Mother and son doing well." Now my chest expanded, and I watched the buttons fly off my shirt into a swarm of mosquitoes, killing several. I now had a son, and he had my name. I was so happy to be alive with a family of five.

Adventures were not pursued; they just seemed to happen.

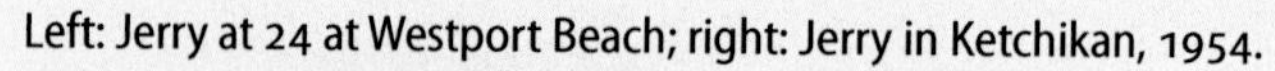
Left: Jerry at 24 at Westport Beach; right: Jerry in Ketchikan, 1954.

I lived in Wrangell, Alaska, with my family. It has always been my favorite spot to remember, because I had a family there with me. I sent them out to visit Gramma for Christmas down in Washington. I was to join them later. On my way to the airport out of Ketchikan, I rode in the jump seat on a Grumman Goose. Coming down on the runway in Metlakatla the landing gear folded under, and we crash-landed. No injuries. My guardian angel rides with me.

I was offered but refused a ride in a new Cessna 185 from Ketchikan to Wrangell. I had a bad feeling, so I said, “No thanks, you guys go ahead. I’ll see ya’ll in Wrangell.” The Cessna crashed and killed two of the three.

Within two years, my wife found someone else.

My family was destroyed.

I became a commercial diver after I moved to Kodiak, Alaska. I worked for Marion Parker, the owner of Aleutian Divers for nine years. Ten years after I arrived in Kodiak, I married Joann Blake. We were married for 40 happy years. Cancer took her from me.

As years pass, my empty life is fulfilled.

A family friend of 40 years thought she could tolerate this 80-year-old. Her family heritage was Icelandic. Vala Hallgrimson became my wife. Shortly after that she got sepsis and was close to death. One year in hospitals and medical care facilities. I was with her every day. She had several amputations. She lost a foot, a leg, all fingers on her right hand and most of her left hand. She is my kind of woman—a fighter, fearless, and part Viking warrior. She has the most positive attitude of anyone I know. She is my love and my inspiration.

Maybe all should realize
Doesn’t matter your size.
To do what you desire.
Just do it before you expire.

Jerry Tilley Sr.

PART I

CHART SERIES
NORTH PACIFIC OCEAN
WEST COAST OF NORTH AMERICA
UNITED STATES – CANADA
DIXON ENTRANCE TO UNIMAK PASS
1:3,500,000 (22°30')
MERCATOR PROJECTION
NORTH AMERICAN DATUM OF 1983
(WORLD GEODETIC SYSTEM 1984)
DEPTHS IN METERS
HEIGHTS IN METERS
AUTHORITIES
Hydrography and topography by the United States National Ocean Service, Coast Survey, with additional data from the United States Corps of Engineers and United States Coast Guard.
COOK INLET
KENAI PENINSULA
ALASKA PENINSULA
KODIAK ISLAND
AFOGNAK I
Shelikof Strait
SHUMAGIN ISLANDS
SHUMAGIN BANK
ALBATROSS BANK
PORTLOCK BANK
TRINITY ISLANDS
PATTON SEAMOUNT
NORTH PACIFI
CONTINUED ON CHART INT 50

1
Ice the Savior

Under normal conditions November in and around Kodiak Island, Alaska, is windy, wet, at times very cold, and usually snowing sideways. Wind velocities were clocked at the Naval Air Station in Kodiak in November of 1962 at 128 mph. At those speeds, chill factors are off the scale, and those who must go fishing to pay the bills are not spending a lot of time worrying about a chill factor. (As a matter of fact, I'm not too certain that back in 1962 anyone knew what a chill factor was. I had never heard of it.)

In 1962, I had just turned 30. My friend Skip got a job on this boat and talked me into joining the crew. I was just another deck hand on an 80-foot, house-forward (the wheelhouse was on the front end of the boat), wooden shrimp fishing boat named *Hekla*. It was not a well-maintained vessel as far as the mechanical functions were concerned, though the living area was tolerable and reasonably clean. The *Hekla* was owned and captained by a 64-year-old hard-ass Icelander who had no fear of the sea, cold, rain, wind, ice, King Neptune, Davey Jones, or the Norse god Odin. Our crew consisted of Captain (he insisted on being called "Captain") Magnus Magnusson, Johnny Martin (the captain's young friend from Bellingham, Washington), Skip Greene, and me, Jerry Tilley. The last two of us were Kodiak residents.

Skip and I had been friends since our days working together in Wrangell, Alaska. We had worked together for about five years. I moved to Kodiak in January 1960, and Skip followed a year later.

Skip and I spent some time in the engine room, and a thought crossed my mind that if anything required lubrication, all we would have to do was start the main engines (two older 671 Detroit diesels that leaked copious quantities of oil), close the hatch for a few minutes, and everything in the engine room would be lubricated. The floorboards and bulkheads were saturated with oil, and so was everything else. We attempted to clean it to a point, then decided it was hopeless in the allotted time. We gathered some cardboard boxes from the grocery store, cut them up to fit, and covered the floorboard sections so we wouldn't track the oil and other miscellaneous residue up to the galley and through the rest of the boat. This course of action seemed to be a clever idea at the time. It even improved the looks of the engine room.

When it was time to go fishing we left our calm moorage in the boat harbor at Kodiak, moved under a cannery's ice chute, and sprayed a 10-inch-deep layer of flake ice on the fish hold bottom. We then filled the square of the hatch to the top of the bin boards. The square of the hatch is the opening six feet square from the deck to the fish hold. We sealed the hatch with the hatch covers, covered them with waterproof canvas, and secured the deck for travel.

Skip was the cook because he was the only one on board who could cook on the oil-fired range without burning the food and the galley to a crisp. The captain always bought the groceries for the trip because he took part of the larder home to feed him and his 21-year-old schoolteacher wife. He took the total cost out of the crew share. We were a little slow to realize that we were paying for a helluva lot more than we were eating. There was usually just enough food for the trip and no extras.

After the fourth or fifth meal of chicken, regardless of how it was prepared, we were ready for a change. The captain would cook us one of his specialties, which consisted of a fresh cod cleaned and the flesh rolled up into little round balls. This was what he called "Norskie cod balls." Properly cooked they were not too bad. Unfortunately, properly cooked cod balls were a rarity because the captain would prepare them, put them on the stove, and then go up in the wheelhouse and fall asleep. We would be working on deck sorting, washing, and icing the shrimp into the fish hold and look up and see black smoke billowing like a volcano eruption from the gal-

ley door. Skip would rush in and grab the pot and throw the round cinder blocks overboard. Then we would eat a chicken sandwich.

We left Kodiak harbor heading east, then southwest to the fishing area through Sitkalidak Straits. It was about 80 miles to the Two Headed Island grounds where we fished. We arrived near the fishing area and anchored amongst the other shrimp boats in Japanese Bay. The weather was about normal for the area in November. There was a big swell and some wind chop, just enough for me to lose the last three meals consumed on flat ground. I always gorged myself when in town, because I knew there was no chance of anything staying down once we started jumping the wave crest and diving to the bottom of the trough with crashing walls of green water inundating the entire vessel. There were few times that I recall when we had a smooth sailing to or from the fishing grounds. After all, this was November in the Gulf of Alaska.

We usually fished for three days and then turned the pointy end of the boat towards Seward on the mainland, where our market was located. It required a run a little south of and across the Barren Islands and the Gulf of Alaska and into Resurrection Bay. When in the ebb (tide going out) in Cook Inlet, the sea flows into the Gulf of Alaska and roars past the Barren Islands. When the wind is from the south or western quadrant, and Cook Inlet ebbs its 30-foot tides in six hours, this area of the Gulf can be extremely treacherous, with mountainous waves and foaming breakers.

We rolled out of our bunks a couple hours before daylight so we could eat breakfast, don the proper attire, and get the gear ready to fish. The wind caused the riggin' to sing and snap with an occasional gust that would let us know this was not going to be a nice day to be sliding across the deck trying to lasso a net full of shrimp. Our captain paid no attention to our comments about the weather, the wind, the swells, or any other lame excuse we could think of prior to hauling the anchor. When the winch was engaged the anchor came up unencumbered just like it was designed to do. We had hoped it would be hung up on a rock or buried in a crevice. No such luck.

We mentioned the fact that none of the other boats had hauled anchor or left the protection of the secluded bay. Captain had selective hearing and was blind to the numerous facts presented by the three of us.

We fished all day in nasty weather. The old *Hekla* managed to stay on top of most of the swells and under a few of them. The boat rolled in the heavy swell. The captain was supposed to try and hold the boat into the swell while we hauled the shrimp aboard. The shrimp bags—known as the cod end of the net where the shrimp end up after the tow is completed—came aboard swinging from the hauling rail all the way across the deck to the other rail and beyond. When that bag of shrimp came aboard, you had to grab the puckering string to empty the contents so the shrimp dropped on the wood grated deck that served as our sorting table. It required lucky timing. However, sometimes the bag's puckering string jerked, and the bag sailed out over the opposite rail and all the contents dumped back into the sea. The puckering string, the line looped through the rings on the bottom of the bag, needed to be tied in a knot to keep it closed while being towed on the bottom.

We managed to catch about 20 tons from daylight to dark, then we headed back in to anchor up for the night. Not one of the other boats had left the bay. We worked most of the night sorting, washing, and icing the shrimp from the last tow. The temperature was close to freezing and my fingers were numb, and my nose was raw from wiping away the drips with my icy gloves. At night on deck sorting and washing the shrimp from the day's catch, all I thought about is how good my bunk was going to feel when I finally crawled into its inviting warmth. The wind was still howling when we hit the sack after midnight.

Another day arrived despite the need for more sleep and staying warm. Four hours just didn't quite do it. The wind had not abated. As a matter of fact, it had increased in velocity, and we were in a protected bay. Our morning whining and complaining about the conditions we were about to encounter had absolutely no effect on our Icelander captain. Weather reports according to Captain Magnusson were never correct anyhow. He always said, "If you want weather reports, start the mains and haul the anchor." We did just that.

We fished another day with the same nasty conditions as the previous day returning to the protected waters of the bay where all the other boats remained at anchor. Not one of them ventured out into the turbulence Mother Nature had conjured.

The third and final day was the one we always looked forward to, because we could rest on the way to Seward. However, this day was no better, and the wind had not reduced its velocity. The riggin' was still screaming and the temperature was dropping and our cries of forced labor and undue hardship in the face of Mother Nature's wrath went unheeded. The captain's hearing had not improved. At breakfast, the captain made the statement, "I can't understand why these other boats don't get out there and fish." We knew the answer to that. None of them were born and raised on a boat in Iceland that fished the North Atlantic.

Up anchor and out to the grounds in big rolling seas and fierce winds. We managed to haul in another big catch for the day with extreme difficulty, as the wind and swell had picked up considerably. We sorted and washed the shrimp, then iced it in the hold. We always iced our shrimp heavy, more so than the boats that had a market in Kodiak. They only had a 5-hour run to unload. We had to travel across the Gulf of Alaska to Seward and, depending on weather, this trip could stretch out from 18 to 24 hours.

Daylight had left and the darkness covered the violence of the sea. My wheel watch was first, and all I wanted to do was hang my head over the rail and unload the last of my intake of food. I looked out through the portholes. All I saw was white combers and green water crashing over the wheelhouse. I had to cut the throttles back to about three-quarter speed. Our portholes were the only reason there was no water in the wheelhouse. The glass was one-half inch thick and each porthole was only twelve inches in diameter. If we had regular wheelhouse windows, they would have been blasted out long ago. With no flood lights, I couldn't see what was coming. I just tried to maintain the compass course. The wind had increased considerably—and it had already been too severe before. The seas were building, and the boat was climbing up the crest and, as the crest broke over the top, we dropped to the bottom with a shudder that felt as if the boat was shaking off the water like a dog. Unfortunately, our course had to change, otherwise we would be broadside to the sea. Conditions continued throughout my 3-hour watch as ice formed on the portholes. My watch ended. Temperatures dropped even more. I got Skip to come and relieve me. After each watch, it was necessary to check the engine room before we crawled into our bunk. I checked it out and all appeared to be OK.

I wedged myself into my bunk and tried to stay in it. My bunk was located fore-and-aft on the passageway from the galley to the wheelhouse. Sleep was out of the question. As the boat climbed a large swell, my feet hit the bottom end of the bunk, and then, when we cascaded to the bottom, my head hit the top end of the bunk. The captain might have been sleeping, but I doubted it. Skip had the watch and was hanging on to the wooden helm. Johnny was in the galley hanging on to the table. We heard from the marine radio that wind speeds had reached 128 miles per hour. It was going to be a very long night.

The portholes in the wheelhouse were totally frozen over with ice, and we barely heard above the screaming wind and crashing seas something tear loose from the top of the wheelhouse. We didn't know if it was chunks of ice or part of the boat. Then the radar quit working, so we thought the radar antenna had parted company. The glass shield on the flying bridge was gone, as it had been replaced by accumulating ice. We no longer were receiving radio communications because the radio antenna had broken off. Our wind gauge pegged out at the max and evidently went with the wind. It only went to 100 miles per hour anyway. We looked out the back door leading from the galley and saw ice building up on the railing and drag door stanchions. The rails had accumulated about a foot of ice so far.

Finishing his watch, Skip handed over the helm to the captain, made his way aft and opened the hatch to the engine room to check it out. I had just crawled out of my bunk and was hanging on when Skip hollered out that the sea was also on the inside of the boat, was rising rapidly, and was sloshing up to the main engines. He and I jumped down into the cold sea water to see why the automatic bilge pump wasn't working and why the bilge alarm hadn't screeched out a warning. Our attempt at covering the floorboards with cardboard to keep the oil in the engine room and not all over the upper decks presented another problem. The water had dissolved the cardboard, washing it off the deck plates into the bilge, and the pumps sucked up the loose pieces, which plugged the entire system. I dove down to the intake on the bilge pump, and the water was rising fast. We had to keep it from reaching the main engine intakes, but I couldn't clear the pump.

By now the water was coming in fast, and we saw the reason after a quick search. The boat was so heavily laden with ice that the dry seams, normally above the water line, were now below it and leaking profusely. The severe pounding by the huge seas had loosened the caulking in the seams, and they were no longer watertight! The water was sloshing from port to starboard, fore and aft, and almost up to both main engines' oil fill pipes. I climbed up out of there soaked with freezing seawater and hollered to Johnny to get us some buckets—right now! I grabbed one bucket and dropped it down through the 24-inch square hatch to Skip, he scooped up a bucketful and reached up over his head. I reached down and grabbed the bail (handle) of the bucket and hauled it up out of there with my right hand and handed it to Johnny. I was on my knees leaning down with one arm to grab the bucket and using the other arm to maintain balance, so I was lifting and reaching out with one arm to hand Johnny the bucket. We had two 5-gallon buckets and one 3-gallon bucket. A gallon of water weighs 8.3 pounds, and the average weight of each bucket was probably somewhere between 20 and 30 pounds, depending on how much was left after Skip scooped it up and handed up to me. Johnny took a couple steps and pitched it out the galley door. I handed another bucket to Skip and scooped up another and held it over his head, and then I reached down to grab it and hand to Johnny, who then pitched it out the door.

Soon the freezing seawater was up to Skip's knees. I asked him if he wanted me to spell him off, and his typical non-verbal response was zero. He just passed me another bucket and kept that up as fast as could. So the bucket brigade never slowed down.

Johnny yelled, "Hey, Jerry, the deck gratings are gone! And the ice is building up around the wheelhouse!"

The ice was nearly three feet thick everywhere. The boat was sluggish to the extreme in the rolls and pitching. Skip and I couldn't stop to chop ice, because the water in the engine room was not going down fast enough. Skip still struggled with bailing, the water rising over his knees. I couldn't believe a man could stand in freezing water for that long without relief. I asked him again if I could spell him off, and I received the same reply—*zero*. Another bucket slapped into my hand. I thought, *this man is one tough guy or dead below his crotch.*

The oil-fired galley range had stopped working. Obviously, the wind blew out the fire. Ice was starting to creep in the galley doorway, freezing the spilled water from our bucket brigade, and making it more difficult to step out far enough to throw the bucket of water. But I had to let Johnny worry about that. It didn't stop him from being the talkative one on board. He never shut up! We accused him of being vaccinated with a phonograph needle. However, he was reasonably quiet while dumping the buckets out the door. Maybe it was because of the howling wind that we didn't hear him.

I was wondering what in the hell I was doing on this coffin of ice. Wondering was about all anyone could do at the time. There were no alternatives. I don't think there were 12 words spoken in the 12 hours that we bucketed water out of the engine room. We didn't stop for even a minute. Bucket down, bucket out. Bucket down, bucket out. Bucket down, bucket out.

We had about 65 tons of shrimp in the hold plus about 10 tons of flake ice. That kept us low in the water. The ice that was forming all over topside added more weight. If this boat had a wheelhouse above the fo'c'sle we most certainly would roll over. The top of the house was only about 6 feet above the aft deck and about 4 feet above the forward deck where the anchor winch was located. On top of the wheelhouse there was only an open flying bridge.

The ice was solid from the bow stem to the top of the wheelhouse and along the rails. Outside the railings, ice was so heavy that large sections would break off as we hit the bottom of a trough. We would drop 30 to 40 feet off the crest and crash to the bottom as we began another swell, then slowly be lifted up for the next one to drop us. The tops of the foaming waves were blown flat from the wind.

We were being blown north, close to the Barren Islands, halfway between the Kenai Peninsula and Kodiak Island. The Cook Inlet ebb was causing massive swells. Some of them were over 50 feet! Our 80-foot *Hekla* would climb a wave for what seemed like an eternity at a 45-degree angle pointing skyward—sometimes—then finally she'd reach the top to cascade down the other side with the stern high in the air. At times we would drop over so fast the prop would come out of the water, and then down we would slide to the bottom of the trough. Another swell would just break over us and the boat would drop and hit with a bone-jarring crash. One of those sudden stops caused the battery racks to pull off the forward bulkhead and partially submerge under the seawater. Miraculously they did remain in operation.

Skip was still passing the buckets without one single minute of variation in the procedure.

Captain stayed at the wheel and never said one word. I guess everyone was deep in their own thoughts wondering if we were going to join the others before us beneath the surface of the sea in Davey Jones' locker, or stay on the surface. I was hoping my guardian angel worked overtime and was fearless.

We no longer had radio or radar, so there was no way to call anyone. It wouldn't have done us any good anyway. No planes were going to be flying, and no vessel of any description was crazy enough to put to sea in this weather. I suppose the adrenaline kept us going, that and the fact that we did not have a life raft. We did have what is referred to as "life vests." The life vests were probably purchased at some military surplus store. They looked like WWII vintage. I wouldn't call them life preservers, because all they could possibly be good for is maybe keep your body afloat long enough for someone to find the frozen remains. These were the kind you used to see in old war movies. They were filled with kapok, which was something like balled up cotton. Newer vests had cork filling that didn't soak up water. In this freezing sea we wouldn't stay alive long enough to realize we were already dead.

Daylight found us north of Marmot Island, which is 40 miles north of Kodiak. In 12 hours we had been blown a hundred miles off course. All we knew was we could see land out the galley door. Captain Magnusson had to come out on deck just to see where we were, then back on the helm. We had to holler to him on where to steer the boat to an acceptable anchorage as the wheelhouse windows were solid ice—and not the kind you can see through.

Our spirits lifted considerably. Captain managed to maneuver the boat into a cove out of the giant seas, affording some protection from the wind. We couldn't stop the bucket brigade yet, so we continued our bailing efforts. At precisely 12 hours of non-stop bailing with buckets we managed to get the water level down below the oil pans of the mains. Venturing out on deck we saw what condition we were in, an iceberg with a mast and 2 stanchions with drag doors tightly secured and covered with ice. The rest of the deck was clean, and the hatch covers were still in place. No water entered the hold. This was a real stroke of luck.

With daylight came some relief from the cold. At least we were not making ice. We were happy to be alive! I was soaking wet and was not aware of the cold. Skip was soaking wet and should have been dead or frozen from the crotch down. He is a born Alaskan and he's tough. Skip is the most stoic individual I have ever known and never has too much to say about anything. If someone tells a joke that makes you fall out of your chair in hysterics, Skip may smile and offer a grunt. Adrenaline had kept us going. We were aware that if we had stopped bailing, the sea water would have covered the engines, and we wouldn't have been able to keep the bow into the sea. The lights would have gone out, and we knew what came next.

Our next move was to try and get the anchor down. We couldn't even get to the anchor or forward around the wheelhouse because it was solid ice. The alternative was to break the drag doors loose and drop them to the bottom and hope they held us in place until we could get rid of some of the ice and survey the damage. After about an hour, we managed to get the doors loose and drop them to the bottom. We waited for a while before patting ourselves on the back, in case the doors didn't hold us in place. The wind had died down, but it was still howling.

We determined that the reason we hadn't capsized and sunk was the thickness of the ice outside the hull, the weight of the water in the engine room and the weight of the shrimp catch in the main hold—decent ballast. We had maintained an even keel, but we realized when the boat rolled, the ice on the outside of the railings and hull kept the rails from rolling under the water. Ice floats and that's a good thing. Lots of spray over the boat, and some of our half-inch cables hanging from the riggin' were now 12–14 inches in diameter. The equipment on the top of the house was gone, as well as the antennas and wind screen on the flying bridge.

We managed to get the stove working, though the only thing left to eat was a packaged cake mix. We baked it and ate it right out of the pan. Recall, our thrifty shopper captain never bought more than a trip's worth of groceries. If not for the 20-plus hours of no-gain travel, we would have been in Seward eating something besides chicken and cod balls.

We still had to get across the Gulf to Seward to unload our shrimp. After an inspection of the hold, we were gratified to see the shrimp still well iced and no seepage through the hatch covers. The temperature kept the ice from melting both in the hold and on the top of the boat. We retrieved a couple buckets of shrimp from the hold and boiled them on the stove. We had us a genuine old-fashioned shrimp feed. We even let the captain have some!

We started chopping ice, but concluded the boat was steady in place and the wind had momentarily died down. We were exhausted. We hit the bunks for a few hours before we continued our attack on the remaining ice. Temperatures had warmed to a point that caused the ice to drop off the railings and the hull. We charged forward to remove the ice from the front of the wheelhouse, the anchor, and anchor winch.

We hauled our drag doors up and secured them to the stanchions. The mains were running, the pumps were cleared, the batteries were back in place, and the cardboard that we could gather up from the oil-covered bilge was deposited in the sea, oil slick and all. Then we departed for Seward on the sixth day out of Kodiak Harbor.

We had to get across the Barren Islands to Rocky Pass on the mainland while the weather and tide were in our favor. We arrived about 12 hours later just before another screaming southwester hit the area. We had to drop anchor and wait it out because

Trying to clear some of the ice while it was steady enough to stand upright on deck.

no one, not even our illustrious, fearless Captain Magnusson, would tempt this pass in the dark. We were very fortunate the anchor held. We ate more shrimp, smoked cigarettes, and drank coffee.

Daylight arrived right on time, about 9:30. We went forward to haul the anchor. It didn't want to leave just yet. It was hung up, and we were certain it wasn't an unknown creature of the deep, but rather a bottomless crevice or a big rock. We backed 'er down and pulled around, forward, reverse, let out cable, haul in cable. Finally, after the captain made the last call, we chopped the cable off, said a few kind words to our only anchor and chain, then waved goodbye. Now we were at the mercy of the gods, as we had no anchor and a questionable bilge pumping system and a fearless captain.

Day seven we were back out into the nasty weather trying to get to Seward. We had no communications with anyone, so if they called the *Hekla* there'd be no answer. The boats that were still anchored in the bay from where we left were aware of our departure date.

Unbeknownst to us we were listed as lost at sea!

We finally arrived in Seward on the morning of the eighth day out of Kodiak. We pulled up to the dock and tied up. We still had some remnants left over from the storm and some ice hanging here and there. The dock crew was in shock when they saw us. They told us we were listed as lost at sea. We agreed with them—*we were lost at sea*. But we never thought about leaving the boat. As I said before, "What was the alternative?"

We hammered the blocks out of the hatch angle irons that kept the canvas cover in place, removed the hatch covers, and dropped down into the hold to see if the shrimp were still a saleable product. Under normal conditions, five days would be a maximum time that you could keep shrimp, providing it was properly iced. We were extremely lucky on this trip. The shrimp were still in good condition, and our catch was accepted by the cannery. The cold temperatures maintained the desired requirement for good product. It was as if we had a refrigerated hold.

As the dock crew proceeded to offload the shrimp, Skip, Johnny, and I headed for the nearest restaurant to attempt filling the void in our stomachs. Captain was probably calling his young wife in Kodiak to tell her we were delayed by inclement weather and to order more chicken. He was the only man aboard that had a wife. Skip, Johnny, and I didn't even have girlfriends.

The return trip to Kodiak after the offload was not much better. Seward was so cold, the water in Resurrection Bay was smokin'. When the water temperature is warmer than the air, fog rises, and it looks like the water is smoking. Kodiak was normally warmer than Seward, so by the time we returned to Kodiak all the ice was gone.

People we met were shocked to see us, because the local paper had reported we had been lost at sea.

Repairs were the order of the following week, and when all was back in shipshape, and the larder was filled with chicken, we made ready for the next trip.

Why did Skip and I return to the boat for the next trip? Adventure? Living on the edge, adrenaline rush, chicken diet? Who knows? We did know it certainly wasn't the big bucks or the meals of those cod balls or the chicken epicurean delights. I reckon we obviously had no clue. It was just something you accept when your living is made on the sea.

Ice Poem

Do I really want to go back to sea?
My partner said come on with me
We will shrimp and make some money
The boat was not a honey
Nothing else to do this time of year
I said okay is there anything to fear
The trip was not expected
Mother Nature determined this boat
Should be rejected
Try as she might throughout the night
She shouldered us with tons of ice
Tried to sink us once or twice
Thank you, tons of ice.

2 What's Down There?

When a diver jumps off a pier or boat or deliberately falls over backwards from a floating Zodiac, they never know what lurks in the water below the surface. A diver submerges into the unknown depths of surprises. If you are claustrophobic or fear the water other than in a bathtub, this life is not for you.

A diver can be a sport diver, an occasional recreational diver, or a commercial diver. I am a commercial diver, which means I work underwater. I have air tanks rather than a hose connected to an air compressor pumping air from above the surface to my mask. That is referred to as a Hookah Air system. The Hookah system hose length restricts the distance you can travel underwater, and it can tangle on debris if you are working on a sunken vessel or other equipment. The only advantage is you can stay underwater longer—if the air compressor doesn't run out of gas.

I have raised sunken vessels, drowned bodies, and lost watches. I have jumped off piers, boats, float planes and ice packs, and out of helicopters. I have welded underwater and sealed cracks in the hulls of vessels. I have constructed underwater intakes and discharging pipelines for the processors operating in Kodiak and Dutch Harbor. I have blown up rocks in the harbor to make way for vessels to get to the docks for offloading without damaging the bottom of the boat. What I enjoy most is jumping out of a helicopter into the ocean below, and the next thrill is blowing things up above and below the water.

Between Kodiak Island and Near Island, I was working underwa-

ter at a depth of 75 feet on a framework that would hold a pipeline discharge system for a processing plant. I was carefully aligning a pipe flange to the steel framework that I had just installed and anchored to the bottom, when for some unknown reason I turned around and looked into the murky water, only to see a large shark slowly swimming by about 20 feet out from my position. I had been diving in Alaska waters for about 10 years and at that point had never seen a shark. As a matter of fact, I didn't know sharks swam around in the icy waters of Alaska.

Now my brain decided to start processing what I had just seen. I knew if I told anyone I just saw a shark, I could visualize the following scene: They would look at me with disbelief, then a smirk just before laughter erupted, and then slap their knee and exclaim, "That's a good one, Jerry, did you see a mermaid riding on it?" Okay, now that I had that thought hanging on, I knew I better do something about it. I swam out to this fat slow-moving shark, retrieved my trusty razor-sharp knife from its scabbard, got alongside the shark, stuck the knife into its side right behind the gills, and made a 2-foot-long slit. It immediately started thrashing around and rolling over as its innards floated out. Afraid it would get away, I quickly swam over to the framework I was working on, untied one end of the line that was attached, and as fast as I could kick my flippers I returned to the thrashing shark that had stirred up the bottom to a point that I could barely see. Somehow I managed to secure the line around its tail and returned to my original position to wait for this monster to die and sink to the bottom. It took longer than I thought it would, but the line held, keeping that shark from drifting out of sight.

Now I had a dead 7-foot-long fat shark lying on the seabed. How was I gonna get this thing up to the float? Grabbing the line I had tied to the tail, I proceeded to drag it, only to find that dead sharks do not drag easily. I finally managed to get it close to where I had been working. I decided to cut off the head, thinking that would be proof enough for any doubting individuals. I tried to stick my knife into the skin right behind the jaw so as to cut around the whole head. The idea died a sudden death. I could not penetrate the skin with the same knife I had used to cut the gash that killed the monster.

The tender on the float above me was awaiting word from me as to what would be needed next to finish the project. My friend Scotty was somewhere north of the 50 mark in age, but still very active. He couldn't see down to where I had been working, so he was just standing by. I surfaced and told him to get me a hand saw.

He looked at me and said, "A hand saw? What are you gonna use a hand saw for on an iron frame and steel pipe?"

I didn't tell him why, I just repeated the statement. He turned around and headed up the float. It must have been a half hour before he returned with the saw. I grabbed it and sank to the bottom where the body was tied off. It wasn't the fault of the knife that I had used. It was the adrenaline surging through my body when I decided to take the chance of killing it. That same adrenaline had somehow returned to its resting place until needed. Seeing as I couldn't cut it up with the knife, I started sawing on it until I had the head severed from the rest of the body. Under normal circumstances I would never think of what I was about to do, but seeing as this was not a normal circumstance, I grabbed the head, which was about a foot and a half in diameter, and opened the mouth as far as it would go. Holding its jaws open and over my head, I planted my flippers on the bottom, crouched down, and pushed upwards to the end of the float where Scotty was standing looking down. The head broke the surface with the mouth full of teeth in full display.

Now, Scotty was extremely quick for an older guy. He turned so fast he fell to his knees and crawled away at full gallop. At that point, his sense of humor was nowhere in the vicinity. I managed to get the shark's head up on the float, spit out my mouthpiece, and set to laughing, expecting Scotty's prolonged tirade of expletives to fill the atmosphere. I didn't have to wait long.

Practically in shock, Scotty demanded, "Where in the hell did you get that thing?"

I explained the whole story and why I needed the saw.

Scotty wasn't too impressed.

Later, I finished up what I was doing below, crawled out on the float, picked up the shark's head and deposited it in the back of my pickup truck. I had a hundred-pound wolf for a pet, and Wolf always rode in the back of the truck, but this time he wouldn't jump in with that shark head lying there. I let Wolf sit in front with me.

As we drove home, my brave Wolf kept looking out the back window at that head.

I stopped by the Alaska Department of Fish and Game to find out what kind it was. We all went outside to the truck, opened the jaws wide and counted 300 teeth in 3 rows. The serrated teeth were about three-eighths of an inch long and about as wide. Initially they didn't know what kind of shark I had, so they got their books out and decided that it was a mackerel shark. I recalled that the shark had been full of salmon and I mean *full*! I couldn't get my arms around the belly. That's why it was so heavy that I couldn't get it out of the water.

I carried that head around on a stake in the back of the truck until the smell got so bad I had to discard it. Anyway, Wolf would still not get in the back of the truck if that head was there. I had to wash the truck bed with detergent and hose it out until there was no odor before Wolf would take up his usual place once again.

What's Down There?

Wet suit, flippers, weight belt and knife
Do I jump in? You bet your life
Wait
How do I know what lurks below
He pushes me in and says, "Now you'll know"
To the bottom
It's really dark and I can't see
Yoweee, yoweee, something's pulling me

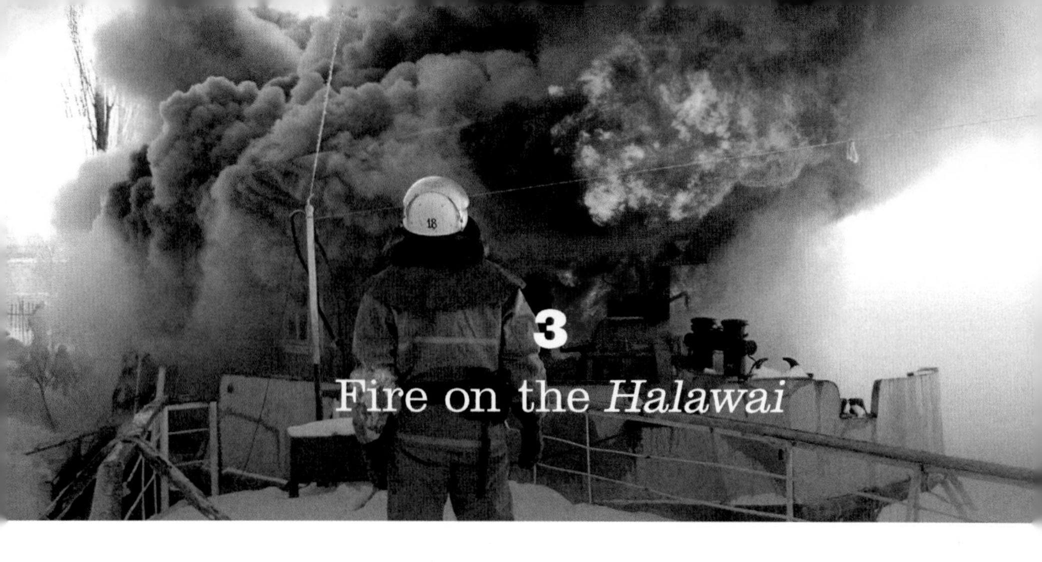

3
Fire on the *Halawai*

Jim Posse and I tied the *Halawai* to the city dock in Juneau and got all our riggin' set to offload when "Fire" rang out. There was a fire in the engine room! It wasn't a raging inferno yet, but engine rooms can become infernos in minutes. All that was needed was air.

Someone must have called the fire department, because they were already on board, across from the engine room door with a 2-inch hose charged with water, ready to go in with the hose nozzle in the closed position.

The fire chief asked me, "Where are the fuel tanks?"

I told him, "You are standing on them."

The firefighters dropped the hose and left the boat.

This event transpired in 1954, when I was hired to design and build a Dungeness crab processing line on an 85-foot power scow named *Josie*. A power scow is built like a barge, with a flat bottom and a large open flat deck with a wheelhouse across the stern. All power scows were built to haul salmon from the fishing boats to the canneries. They have two main engines and living quarters for four and a captain's stateroom. The galley is on the second deck. Jim Posse and I were hired by Roy Furfiord, the owner of both boats, to bring the scow from Tacoma to Westport.

The *Josie* was still in Tacoma, Washington, tied up to a vacant pier. The *Josie* had been there for quite some time. The paint was peeling and the exposed deck planks had dried out, revealing the oakum caulking. Oakum caulking is driven into the cracks between planks to seal the seams and make them watertight. Jim Posse, the chief engineer, and I were sent to Tacoma to get the *Josie* ready to sail. First thing was to repair the two main engines and the pumps. We worked for two weeks, and then we set sail for Westport, Washington. I was at the wheel taking the boat south. The weather was not ideal, and we were taking water over the bow. Jim was in the engine room, working on the bilge pumps to suck out the water that was leaking through the open seams in the deck planks.

We had planned to refit the *Josie* at Chilman Shipyard in Hoquiam, just up-river from Westport. I designed all the equipment that would be installed in the boat while the rest of the work building the deckhouse was in progress. The companion to *Josie* was the freezer ship, *Halawai*, which was tied to a pier in Westport waiting for the work on the *Josie* to be completed. The *Halawai* would be the galley and living quarters for the crew, and its freezer would hold the product that was to be produced.

Space on the *Josie* was limited so I had to be creative. I designed a crab hopper that only required 3 square feet of space and 3 feet off the deck. After everything was finished on both the *Halawai* and the *Josie*, we loaded all the necessary supplies and secured the equipment. We were ready to depart and head north to Yakutat, Alaska, along the coast just north of the inland waters of Southeast Alaska. We departed Westport with the *Halawai* leading off and the *Josie* behind us. There were a total of four crab boats loaded with crab pots that were to fish for us. We followed one another north to Yakutat. We looked like a seagoing train.

On arrival in Yakutat, the *Halawai* tied up to the dock, and the *Josie* moored alongside it to complete the processing production system. The finished product from the *Josie* was transferred to the *Halawai* for freezing and stowage in the freezer hold.

The season was better than we expected, and we filled the freezer hold on the *Halawai* to the point that we had to stop the boats from any more fishing. The *Halawai* then left Yakutat, sailing back south for Cross Sound, the opening to the inside waters of Southeast Alaska. Our destination was Juneau, to unload our crab. We tied up at the Juneau AK Dock, and that's where the fire broke out on the *Halawai*.

Jim grabbed that fully charged hose, opened the engine room door, and dove down into thick black smoke and fire. I backed him up, feeding him the hose. I was careful not to block the opening in case he came charging out for air. Standing outside the entrance to the engine room, I could hardly breathe for the acrid black smoke. Sounds of sizzling filled the air, along with the steam generated from the water hitting whatever was burning. It wasn't but a few minutes and Jim staggered up out of there hackin' and chokin', with a soot-covered face. His one white eye peered out of the smoke at me. Jim only had one eye. He'd lost the other working in a shop when he bent over to pick up something on the floor. He hit a sharp file end that was protruding from the workbench, and the sharpened end penetrated his eye socket.

Jim choked out the words, "The fire is out, I'll be right back." He descended again into the black hole, with me following right behind him. There was still a lot of smoke, but it was clearing, so we could see but could still hardly breathe. We were fortunate because we still had lights. Checking everything to make sure nothing was still burning, we retrieved the fire hose and made sure we were not leaving with it prematurely. I was the first out of the engine room door. Then and only then did I see a fireman. They wanted to make sure we were not going to blow up there at the city dock.

I thought we were out of business for sure. Well, not really. Jim the repair genius, after a review of the damage, said he could do repairs and fix things so we could sail within a few days. But we were going to need a lot of new wiring. Jim is a typical Alaskan who can not only kill fires but repair the damage caused by fires. Wiring is usually the most significant problem. Other than that, aside from burnt wood and everything in the engine room black from smoke, we could sail again without a long shipyard repair.

We offloaded all the product, because it was in the forward freezer hold and a long way from the engine room fire and smoke.

I celebrated my 24th birthday at the Red Dog Saloon, not far from the docks down on South Franklin Street. The Red Dog was one of Juneau's oldest drinking establishments, going back to the early years of the Juneau gold mine discovered by Joe Juneau and Richard Harris in 1880.

We returned to Yakutat. It was September 9, 1955, when I received a radio message from ACS (Alaska Communication System) telling me that I had just became the father of a son. Added at the end: "Mother and son were doing fine." I had so much pride, it was like my chest had expanded so far that the buttons of my shirt snapped off into the cloud of mosquitoes (killing several). I was so happy to be alive and have a family of five.

We had finished a very successful season, even with the delay in Juneau caused by the fire. So Jim Posse and I departed Alaska for Westport with the forward freezer hold full of product. Now you can imagine how anxious I was to get home. We had to take the boat into Seattle, because the owner and I were the only ones capable of handling it in case something went wrong. We had one crewman to help with the wheel watch.

We arrived in Seattle and offloaded our product. My wife arrived, and we drove home to see my son, Jerry "Corky" E. Tilley Jr. He was 6 weeks old when I first saw him.

I picked him up.

And he smiled.

And I cried.

Fire on the *Halawai*

Find a boat that will float in fair shape
Design a process line and don't hesitate
All was completed in a very short time
Tried it out in Alaska and it was a good sign
A slight interruption one day to slow us down
We even survived an unscheduled week in town
Back to Yakutat and work some more
On a ship you never know day to day what's in store

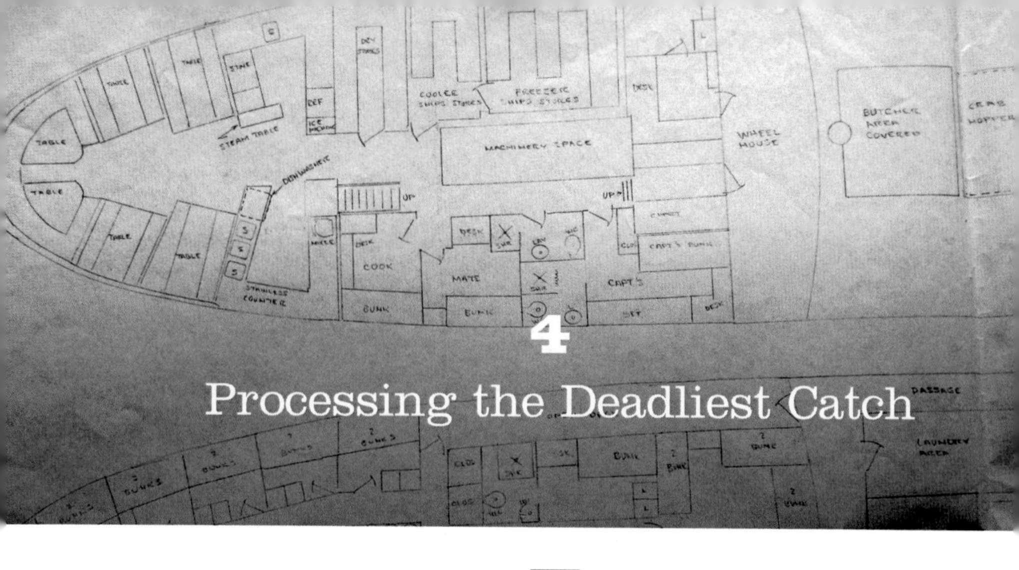

4
Processing the Deadliest Catch

The boats you see on Discovery Channel's *Deadliest Catch* must quickly deliver their haul of crab to processors for processing. That could be a floating-on-board processor anchored in a secluded bay, or the boats may deliver to a shore plant. The advantage of delivering to an anchored floating processor is the time required to travel from their crab pots, also called "gear," to offload. The "gear" are left on the bottom until the vessel returns from offloading. The floating processors have what the boat needs to continue fishing in the shortest time away from their gear. They have bait and fuel and offer a quick turnaround. If the boat has to travel 20 or 30 hours, even a couple of days, to a shore plant, it's the same time to return back to the fishing grounds to pull their pots full of crab. The captains of these King crab fishing boats do not like to deliver to town. They often have to wait for an offload behind other vessels. There are also times the crew sneaks off to the bar for a few quick ones—and they always forget that "quick" doesn't exist after the third or fourth drink.

This is our story: We tie a boat full of crab to the *Akutan*, unload it, fuel it up, then deliver the necessary bait to keep the boat fishing. We cast off the tie-up lines and away goes the boat.

I returned to the *Akutan* in Dutch Harbor. I had just passed a United States Coast Guard test in Seattle that got me a 2000-ton master's license. I took an outboard skiff to the *Akutan*, anchored in the inner harbor, and signed into the ship's logbook that the master had boarded and taken over command of the vessel.

This vessel was purchased for $1.2 million. We brought it to Seattle to Tippet Marine, a shipyard on Lake Union. I had already planned on what was needed for this out-of-date-crab processing ship. The entire weather deck had to be removed along with all existing equipment, and everything hauled to the recycle dump. I designed every piece of deck gear and equipment to be installed, including two 75-horsepower boilers. I had Ershigs in Bellingham make all the fiberglass piping, connecting tanks, and water systems. Fiberglass pipe does not deteriorate, saltwater or acid will not eat a hole in it, cold or hot does not affect it, and you can drill a hole and add a pipe anywhere you want and fiberglass it in place. More expensive than stainless steel, but fiberglass will outlast Methuselah's 969 years.

The F/V *Akutan* was refitted and in shipshape. Now that the newly licensed captain was aboard, we were legally ready to travel head back out to sea. We went to the Bering Sea and west to Kiska.

I told Steve Martin, my chief engineer, to crank 'em up—*we're gonna move*. Marty Hanna, my unlicensed mate, got ready to haul the anchor. We then headed to the fuel dock to top off our tanks for travel. I slowly maneuvered the 180-foot vessel alongside the fuel dock. The hanging anchor hooked a piling. The piling split, causing the bow to hit the bull rail and loosen some planks.

Ah yes! An excellent docking maneuver for my first landing as captain of my own ship.

Marty didn't hawse (secure) the anchor; he just let it hang loose. *Thank you, Marty. You and I will talk later.*

We fueled up and got our groceries loaded aboard.

Three new crew arrived on the plane. One of them came aboard with a ragged pair of pants and a sweatshirt that was no better. I asked the kid if he had any decent looking clothes, and he said that was all he had. It's quite apparent if you are standing upright and breathing, the office hiring personnel will send you to Alaska.

"You are not sailing on this ship

looking like a humanoid reject that just dragged himself off the street," I told him and gave him $150 to buy some decent clothes and then hurry back or we'd leave without him.

The crew finally aboard, we gathered in the galley where I proceeded to give the "indoctrination to living aboard the *Akutan*" presentation. The first topic was safety, and my foreman Marty delivered the "safety and living aboard" program. All personnel received a survival suit and were instructed how to get it on as fast as possible; they had to demonstrate proficiency before we sailed. There were some humorous moments watching these *cheechakos* (new to Alaska) trying to get into their survival suits in less than a minute. Made you wonder how they get their pants on in the morning. Finally, everyone had satisfactorily performed this task.

The next essential item on the safety list was the limited use of water and what not to put in the toilets.

Final instructions completed, we are all headed off to our stations, tie-up lines were released, and we went out of Dutch Harbor into the Bering Sea. Then headed west to Kiska Island out on the Aleutian Island chain. We arrived in Kiska in good shape and ready to begin processing onboard.

The *Akutan*'s twin booms were raised and her two 18-foot aluminum skiffs were lowered overboard out of the way of the incoming King crab boats anxious to unload their catch. Before the boats arrived, we secured two 6-foot long by 3-foot diameter rubber bumpers over the starboard side. When the crab vessel came alongside, the bumpers kept the two vessels from rubbing together as they rocked in the waves.

The first fishing boat eased alongside the *Akutan*, and we tied her up using her mooring lines along with two of our own. The fishing boat's hatch cover was set aside. Then the circulating sea water was pumped out exposing the catch of the live crab.

My unloading crew jumped down into the open

Newly-converted 'Akutan' working well

"It's working beautifully – better than I expected," is the word from Jerry Tilley of Seawest Industries on the rebirth of their 167-foot processor, the **Akutan**.

The vessel has been around since 1964, processing for Pacific Pearl, but last spring Seawest took it to Sea-Land Associates for an extensive conversion.

Tilley will discuss the make-over of the **Akutan** at one of the seminars that will be held as part of Fish Expo '81, which opens Wednesday, Oct. 28, at the Seattle Center. Tilley's seminar will be at 2 p.m. Thursday, Oct. 29.

He estimates he has done 13 or 14 vessel conversions. The boat was stripped from the house bulkhead forward to the forepeak on the main deck. The weather deck was raised four and one-half feet and the mast and cargo booms were moved aft to the front of the wheelhouse, giving a wide-open area from wheelhouse to forepeak.

Hershigs, Inc. of Bellingham constructed fiberglass pipe, which was made in place, between cooker, cooler, chiller and brine freezer. Pipe was installed below the catwalks, connecting the four units.

The processing [illegible] was designed and [illegible]

◄ The newly-converted [illegible] under way in Western Al[illegible]

◄ Coastline Equipment manufactured the processing equip[illegible] AKUTAN, including this stainless steel butchering area.

The AKUTAN's jet rail is a five-inch "I" beam, 48 feet in le[illegible] built in three sections and pinned together with interlocking br[illegible] come a continuous rail. The rail will accommodate 20 trolleys, [illegible] three crab bags. The rail has six supports and they are held i[illegible] pins, which are easily removed. The entire system, crab bags [illegible] dismantled and stored for travel in less than an hour. ▼

hatch, while the boom operator swung the netted bag over the hold, lowering it down to a level that allowed the crew to fill it with the live crab.

The crabs objected fiercely to being handled but lost the battle.

After the net-bag was loaded with crab, it was lifted out of the hold and weighed. One bag usually held about 250 to 300 crabs and weighed between 1,500 and 2,000 pounds. The bag weight was always checked by one of the crab boat's crew to avoid any accusations of our giving them less weight than the scale read. Fishermen never believed the weight unless they saw it with their own eyes. One of their crew stood ready to record the weight reading on the scale.

The full bag was then transferred across the deck, swinging between the twin booms to port side. The top of the bag's mesh tightened, tied, and secured closed, it was hung on the rail, so the top of the closed and secured mesh was below the water. In this way, the crabs think they will be okay. We didn't tell them what came next.

Each bag received the same treatment. When we were ready to process, the crab bag was lowered over the butcher bin and the puckering string pulled, thus opening the bottom of the bag and releasing the crab, where they tumbled into the bin. The butcher grabbed the crab's legs, three legs in each hand, and pushed the belly into a sharpened blade killing it instantly. This procedure removed the carapace (crab back) that contained the heart and guts. Then the two sections of the crab were thrown on the stainless steel table where the gilling machines took over.

One hard-and-fast rule we followed: never process a dead crab regardless of the species. When picked up, if a crab's legs hung down with no apparent movement, it was obviously dead and was discarded overboard, where the sea otters waited noisily for breakfast, lunch, or just a snack. The otters grabbed the crabs, laid them on their stomachs, and cruised around on their backs while leisurely pulling off a leg and eating it. The other otters all shared, and were well fed when we were in the area.

During the butchering process, most of the crab backs went into a grinder to be discharged below the vessel. Sometimes we tossed a few crab backs to the otters. The playful sea otter grabbed the shell, again put it on its stomach, and ate right out of the shell.

The hydraulic gilling machine had a 6-inch diameter stainless-steel toothed roller to de-gill the crabs. Before going below to the packing belt, mud or other debris was pressure-washed away. Then the crab sections were dropped through a hole to the deck, where they landed on a belt ready for the packing crew, who packed the sections into wire baskets. A full basket was weighed for uniformity before being hoisted forward into the cooker, a boiling seawater tank, for about 20 minutes (larger crabs cooked a little longer). The foreman, who answered to the captain, determined cooking times.

After the cooking process, the crab was lifted by a hoist and moved to a cooling tank of continuously circulating seawater, where it stayed until the next basket out of the cooker was ready to take its place.

Next stop, the prechilling tank, was about the same size as the cooker and cooling tanks. The prechilling tank was kept at a temperature just warm enough to keep the water from freezing.

Now the temperature of the basket of crab was cold enough to merge into the brine freezer tank, also identical in size. Brine temperature was kept at zero to 5 degrees below zero. If the brine reached a temperature above 7 degrees the crab would absorb the salt of the brine and make it too salty to eat. Brine tank salinity was

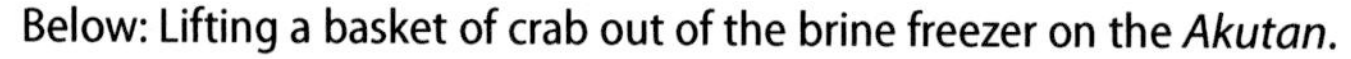

Below: Lifting a basket of crab out of the brine freezer on the *Akutan*.

90% or more. Too low a salinity, or too low a temperature, and the brine got mushy. Therefore it was critical that the workers maintained strict control of each tank, especially the cooking temperature and the brine freezer.

* * *

The process of brine freezing whole Dungeness crabs was started in Westport, Washington, by my dad, Allen Douglas Tilley, back in 1946. (The process of brine freezing sections of crab was not invented for another 20 years.) As far as we knew, no one else was using brine freezing on crab or other shell fish. This process was short-lived, though, when we discovered the crab had to be complete with all legs intact and no breaks in the shell. The brine would enter any opening and saturate the innards with salt, causing the crab meat to be too salty to eat. Also, the crab legs had to be folded next to the body of the crab so they could be packed in a box without breaking off the frozen legs. Therefore, each crab had its legs folded inward and a rubber band attached to hold them in place before freezing.

Maintaining the zero-degree temperature when the crab baskets were submerged in the brine was difficult, until we realized the colder the product was before being lowered in the brine, the better the temperature would hold—and the quicker the product would freeze.

The basket of crab was then moved from the cooling water into the freezer holding room, where the temperature was 32 degrees for a couple of hours before brine freezing. Thus the problem was solved.

The brine freezer worked okay until we brine-froze live, fresh razor clams. Fishermen loved those brine-frozen clams for Dungeness crab bait. That program worked exceptionally well, until the circulation of the brine started to dwindle and then stopped. The prop that was turned by a V-belt attached to an electric motor quit turning, causing the drive belt to start smoking and the entire tank to freeze up. That stopped production of all species.

My dad was always trying something new. It took days for the brine to thaw and dig the frozen clams out of the frozen salt. We learned something on that maiden voyage into brine-freezing razor clams. We opened the drain valve to empty the tank, but nothing came out. We poked a wire in the valve to see what was stopping the flow of brine and all we found was sand. When we eventually got the tank empty of liquid and down to the metal plates that covered the ammonia freezing coils, we could see sand left on the metal plates. The circulating prop located below the plates had stopped, which caused the freeze-up. The reason the prop stopped was evident when we pried the metal plates up. The bottom of the tank was full of sand that covered all the coils and the prop. Lesson learned: when we dumped the clams into the brine, they had time before they realized they were frozen to give themselves about 2–3 pumps as if they were going down in the sand for home. This pumping released all the sand they had in their body. The sand was very hard to dig out. We had to get around the coils in the bottom of the tank and dig out the sand using small shovels and our hands. We learned the hard way, and it put us out of the brine-freezing business for a month. No more freezing razor clams in the brine freezer.

* * *

Back to the *Akutan* processing in Kiska Harbor, way out in the Aleutians among the small group of islands called Rat Islands.

The basket of frozen crab was lifted by hoist out of the brine freezer and lowered into a fresh-water tank for glazing for a half minute, then immediately taken out and lowered onto a table where it was removed from the wire basket. Slipping a plastic bag over the solid block of frozen and glazed crab, the loose ends were folded over, sealing the block. Then a cardboard box was lowered over that, the flaps folded closed, and the box moved to a Signode strapping machine. Two straps later, the box was stowed in the lower freezer hold.

Some of my crew had been with me for years, and I couldn't have asked for better shipmates. My granddaughter Charise joined the crew for a season. She worked the galley with the cook Michelle. She kept the galley clean, washed all the cups, dishes, pots, pans, and kettles. In addition to those duties, she helped the cook prepare meals.

One time she came into the wheelhouse and said, "Grampa, come down and see my galley. I just cleaned everything!"

"Great," I replied. "Let's go!"

The galley looked like a hospital! The stainless-steel countertops sparkled, the freshly mopped deck glistened, and the 6-foot long stove-top shined like new! I walked over to the cup holder that was close to the coffee pot and lifted it. There were a few crumbs and some coffee grounds underneath. Charise was shocked! She backed up with fire in her eyes and shouted—not too loudly however—"Grampa, you're just like my mother."

Where do you think your mother got it? Virgos are terrible about things like this. My mother, my father, my oldest daughter (Charise's mother), my son, my youngest daughter, a grandson, several great- and great-great-grandchildren, and me—we're all Virgos. We like clean and tidy. My dad didn't just like clean and tidy, he insisted on it!

When we were loaded with 200,000 pounds of King crab frozen in 50-pound blocks, we hauled anchor and sailed off to Dutch Harbor to offload our cargo onto a freighter.

Project completed, I moved the *Akutan* to the fuel dock—this time without crashing into it. We fueled up, gathered supplies, and departed once again for Kiska Harbor.

That was life on a processing ship.

And in five years of captaining the *Akutan*, I only hit a dock once.

Processing the Deadliest Catch

The ship waits on anchor with a full crew
Waiting for the captain with license anew
Landing in Dutch on a twin-engine plane
Finally back to the *Akutan* once again
Throw off the lines and get underway
Point this ship west to Kiska Island's bay

5
The Battle with Sea Lions

A commercial diver swimming in water where visibility is near zero most of the year encounters many unknowns. I have had some exciting moments with seals, sharks, sea otters, and sea lions. Only one scary critter that I saw before it saw me was a salmon shark, a species of mackerel shark, big and fat, and obviously well fed. My first encounter with a shark was quite a surprise, actually, as I was not even aware sharks were swimming around in Alaskan waters.

Out in the Aleutians, I have run into seals that appeared curious. I suppose they were wondering what that bubble-producing monster was doing in their fishing grounds. They were not aggressive and just swam around me, staring. Some would stop and look me right in the eye from about 3 feet away.

In Kiska Harbor, way out in the Aleutians past the International Date Line, I had a pet sea otter that followed me wherever I went underwater. It would come up to my mask and stick its nose right in my face. I would reach out and scratch its head, and then it would swim around in circles until I went to the bottom and turned over the big rocks it couldn't move, so it could chase the hiding crabs and other little creatures that called the underside of the rocks their home. When I would get out of the water to change tanks, it would come up and scream until I got back in the water.

I was in Akutan Bay with my ship, also named *Akutan*, a 180-foot seafood processing vessel tied up to the Trident Seafood's dock. The sheet piling was the face of the dock, and some of the sheet pilings appeared to be angling outward at the bottom. Chuck Bundrant was at the plant at the time and asked me to check it out. Aboard my ship I gathered up my diving equipment, donned my diving suit, filled an air tank, and was ready to jump into the icy waters.

Swimming to the end of the dock, I began the survey. The dock was about 400 feet in length, shallow where I started heading east, and getting deeper as I progressed toward the right angle that faced north, the longest section of the dock. Forty feet from the corner I felt something but didn't see anything, because my attention was focused on the bottom of the piling where it entered the sandy surface. Then something hit one of my flippers. Turning sideways, I saw a monstrous sea lion shoot off and make a big turn then head back for another run. It passed within 4 feet of my head, and I forgot all about the pilings.

A moment later, two sea lions zipped by me and circled back again. These critters are not little 300 or 400 pounders, but 6 to 8 feet long—about as big as a Volkswagen Bug at over half a ton—and fast as a hot torpedo!

Minutes passed. I hadn't moved. Finally, when I thought they had had their fun and were nowhere to be seen, I returned to my survey.

But I was wrong. This time something grabbed my fin and pulled it hard enough that I thought it was coming off. Now there were five of these giant sea lions circling me and brushing up against me, mouths agape, as if it was time to eat.

They were starting to piss me off, and as luck would have it I noticed two topping mauls lying nearby on the bottom, obviously dropped there by the sheet piling driver crew. A topping maul is like a sledgehammer with a tapered point on one end and weighing about 4 pounds. I grabbed them up one in each hand and turned around to meet the attack. One came at me, and I planned to put a dent in its head. But it was too fast, and I failed to act quickly enough. But a second one swam in right behind the first for a big bite of my body. This time I managed to get a hit in, but not on the head. Swinging a sledge hammer underwater is a slow-motion procedure, so to be effective the critter would have to run into the hammer.

Another sea lion bumped into me with enough force to slam me against the sheet piling, but then there was a moment's break in the attacks. I decided it was time to make an exit, even as they all decided to pay me another visit. Now I counted six monsters. They were huge! Six Volkswagen Bugs lined up to finish me off. A topping maul in each hand, they came at me for what I figured was the kill. As fast as I could swing them, I slammed the two topping mauls together, and like magic the monsters shot out of there and never returned. The sound of the two hammers clanging together must have hurt their ears, and they wanted no more of me.

With a maul in each hand I managed to climb out of the water and onto the pier. From the top of the dock I could see the sea lions' heads just above the surface about 100 yards out in the bay.

I would have welcomed a herd of killer whales that day. They love sea lions.

The Battle with Sea Lions

How about checking the pilings for me
Okay, I'll dive down and check to see
Not looking away, just at the piling
Happy to dive and no fear as I am smiling
Something hits my flipper
I turn around fast
Then I see it coming, then going past
Then there are five trying to eat me alive

6
Forget the Guitar!

I was working on a liberty ship in Old Harbor on Kodiak Island, setting up a herring roe production line, when a helicopter, piloted by my friend Ron Mosgood flew in, settling down on the small dock where the ship was tied. Out jumped Marion Parker, my diving partner and owner of Aleutian Divers. He informed me that there was an emergency out by Amber Bay, due west of Tugidak Island with an LST (landing ship, tank).

"You've heard about the converted World War II LST that was being used to haul heavy equipment all over Alaska and the Aleutians?" he asked.

"Sure," I said. "What's happened?"

"She's overturned! Three of the crew managed to get off. Were rescued by a boat traveling along with a construction equipment vessel."

Marion had brought all my diving gear with him. He didn't have too many details, just that they needed a diver as soon as one could get out there. I jumped in the chopper, and away we flew to Amber Bay.

A fleet of construction boats and equipment at anchor awaited our arrival. We landed on top of a barge loaded with house trailers, actually atop one of the trailers. The whole operation included a supply vessel, a tug, and barge. We only required the diving details.

Marion and I climbed out of the helicopter and off the house trailer, then boarded the boat that had saved the crew of the overturned LST. Not far off, we could see the bow of that LST sticking up out of the water, being kept barely afloat by an air bubble up at the bow.

The crew explained what had happened. The LST was carrying two Caterpillar D8 tractors, each around 16 tons, two dump trucks, a rock crusher, a road grader, a large air compressor, two conveyors, and a variety of other equipment. They were sailing to Sand Point for a construction project when the LST started rolling in the swell soon after clearing the south end of Kodiak Island. They sought shelter from the rough weather in Amber Bay. Turning into the bay, the LST took a broadside swell causing the vessel to list past the recovery point. List is the degree of the angle which a vessel tilts. The crew had no choice but to abandon ship. However, one young man still in the doorway had yelled that he to go back and get his guitar. The vessel rolled over with him inside.

"He's still in there," said one sailor. "Inside the aft house. He may be trapped in an air pocket in the cabin!"

The old landing craft had 8-foot-high sides all around the vessel. It had capsized with the drop ramp on the bow still in the up position. If the air that was holding the bow up leaked out, the vessel would sink upside down trapping whoever was still inside. An undesirable diving situation at best.

We could see the hull raising and lowering in the swell at the head of the bay about a mile outside of where the others anchored. We retrieved our gear and suited up. Marion had brought what he thought was all my gear except for gloves. But he did think to bring an airbag in case we needed to float something—like a body.

Back in the chopper, we flew out to the LST. Ron held about 30 feet up and alongside the bobbing hull of the LST. Marion got out on the starboard side runner, and I got out on the port side. Face masks and regulators held tight, facing one another, I gave the sign to drop. We both jumped at the same time, hitting the water about 20 yards away from the upside-down hull!

We swam to the port side and dove under, coming up inside the walled-in capsized deck. The two D-8 Cats had broken free and sank. Fortunately, visibility was exceptional, with plenty of light—at least as long as the bow was still afloat. The vessel's bobbing up and down was nerve-wracking. We knew if the air left we could be trapped. The stern house was actually touching the sea-floor.

My hands were icy cold, as I had no gloves. We swam over to the doorway leading into the aft-structure where the crew's quarters and galley were located. Looking into all the staterooms and spaces,

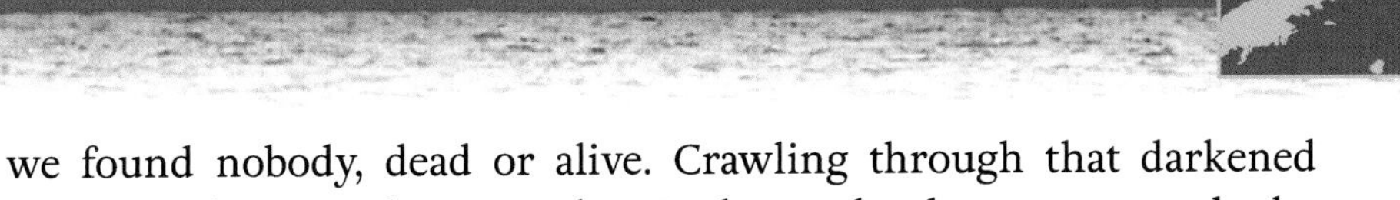

we found nobody, dead or alive. Crawling through that darkened interior cabin tested our resolve. Back out the door, up towards the bow, and out into open water, we finally surfaced.

I hoped the sailor might have made it back to the door and out on his own, maybe the air inside having blown him out. But it seemed he was lost. A life for guitar. Sad!

We were a long way from shore. I estimated about a mile, and spotted the helicopter sitting on a low point of land. Our choices were pretty much run out, with a long swim back to shore. A diver knows it is easier to swim underwater than on the surface, but that only lasted until the air ran out.

We swam for shore underwater, until the air tanks ran out of air. The remainder of that mile swim was exhausting. When we reached the beach, I wasn't sure I could climb the hill to the helicopter. Marion was lying out on the rocks conserving his energy to make the climb up the steep slope to the chopper. I held my flippers in my non-feeling, frozen hands, and we ascended the slippery slope and finally reached the grinning Ron. He told us this was the closest spot to land from the LST. He couldn't pick us out of the rough waters.

Flying back to the trailer house barge, we relayed our sad story and gave details concerning what was left chained to the deck now lying at the bottom of the bay.

Once again in the chopper, we headed back to Kodiak Island, skimming the rock outreaches and chasing the feathers off nesting ptarmigan, Alaska's state bird.

Marion and Ron left me on the dock where my ship was tied up. I told Marion to take care of my gear, and they took off back to Kodiak.

I went to my room and crashed.

Forget the Guitar!

I think I will take a nap, but helicopter lands, so I get no rest
My dive partner says we have an emergency out west
The pilot lifts and we are on our way heading for a bay
A boat rolled over and the crew says there is one you have to save
Upside-down a mile offshore we see the bow above the wave
We leap from the chopper swim under hopefully not to our grave

7
New Hope

The state of Alaska practically closed its doors when the last salmon was packed and the last Dungeness crab was canned. I came back to Westport, Washington, looking for opportunity. In that fishing town, there was some word in the air about a new fishery for shrimp. That was something different, and it got my immediate attention.

Shrimp off the coast of Washington? Out on a boat and after a few test runs and a small net, to my surprise and elation, there appeared to be a good supply of shrimp. Now using a bigger net and a larger boat proved a shrimp industry could soon be developed.

A shrimp peeling machine was being built in New Orleans, Louisiana, by a brilliant engineer named Raphael Quentin Skrmetta, better known as "Ray" Skrmetta. Ray trained on a B-29 Superfortress during World War II, where he improved his engineering talent. After the war, he started Skrmetta Machinery Corporation and used those skills to build the first shrimp peeling machine.

The Kaakinen Fish Company in Westport purchased one of Ray's peeling machines. Probably not the very first peeling machine, but the first one on the coast of Washington.

I knew Ed Kaakinen. I'd worked at his company years before canning tuna and operating the tuna cookers. Ed knew my mechanical abilities and hired me to get indoctrinated on the shrimp peeling machine—and possibly help develop a new industry for the area.

When I first saw this unit, I had no idea what or how it could peel a shrimp, especially the small pink shrimp, the *Pandalus borealis*. Processing machinery of any kind always intrigued me.

I was fascinated by its hundreds of moving parts. What kind of intrinsically brilliant mind could dream up something this complex? My admiration grew. I was hooked on this shrimp peeling device, and was able to get instructions directly from Ray Skrmetta on its operation.

My career expanded with the Kaakinen Fish Company as we started processing shrimp. The first boats to fish for shrimp were new to shrimp fishing, but they had a lot of experience dragging for bottom fish. They would drag and bring the shrimp in with the ocean bottom mud, and we would process. At first, we had some problems with the finished product because of the mud embedded in the shells. We tried a few different procedures to clean the shrimp before going into the peeling machines, but the cleaning was not working a hundred per cent. Something had to change in product deliveries.

I had an idea about how to improve the delivered catch. George Muscovita was captain of the shrimp boat *New Hope*. I asked him if I could go with him on the next shrimp harvesting trip to experiment with a new idea. I asked him if he had a washdown hose on board, and he did, but only a small diameter one. My brainstorm was in high gear. I asked if he could rig up a two-inch hose to his washdown outlet with a hose adapter. He agreed to try out my suggestion, and after a day of changing the washing system, we were ready to go fishing.

The first tow brought up a good load of shrimp. The crew raised the bag then lowered it back into the water a couple of times trying to clear the mud from the shrimp. It was then dumped onto the grating on deck. The crew's job was to wash the shrimp. I grabbed the washdown hose and started washing the shrimp by turning it over by the shovel full and washing until the run-off water was clear. Afterwards, it was shoveled into the hold for icing. The day went well, and we caught several tons of shrimp, all washed clean of mud.

I will never forget that first day and the success we had cleaning the shrimp with more washing and a larger volume of water. It was an extraordinary experience on the *New Hope*.

After cleaning all the shrimp, we hit the sack before another day of fishing.

The next morning before daylight, while lying in my bunk, I

heard George's wake-up call, "Daylight in the swamp, hot dogs and buns and all the mustard you can eat."

After breakfast, we went out on the deck in a thick fog. It was just breaking daylight, and we were getting ready to set the net overboard when the thick fog cleared—like going through a door from near dark to a brighter day.

All of a sudden, we heard high-pitched screaming from the water. Alarmed, all three of us on deck, in addition to George from the wheelhouse, ran to the rail. We were 30 miles offshore west of Westport boat harbor. Nearby floated an 18-foot aluminum skiff with three people aboard, waving their arms frantically and screaming. The woman did most of the screaming. A 25-horse Evinrude was propped up on the transom, and they sat there dead in the water.

George maneuvered the *New Hope* alongside. The woman was hysterical, and her husband seemed to be getting the brunt of it. They had no gas, no water, no food, no life preservers, and no brains. They had been fishing for salmon out of Westport when the fog rolled in over them and everyone else in the area. The husband thought he was steering toward shore, but instead he was heading for Japan when they ran out of gas. They'd been out all night, praying to God for someone to save them. Then out of the fog, the bow of our boat appeared with the name brightly displayed: "New Hope." God had answered their prayers.

The woman unrelentingly inundated her husband with some rather coarse vulgarities. The poor husband had nothing to say in return, and I am sure he knew what was best. The other man in the boat was her brother. He followed the husband's lead in not saying much. I asked the husband if he had a compass. He sheepishly replied, "No." I had no further questions for any of them. You can't fix stupid. Up on the bridge, George was speechless, shaking his head.

There was not another boat anywhere in sight. We loaded them aboard and filled them with coffee. After winching the skiff aboard, then George decided to head into the harbor and unload the three of them and the shrimp.

This day was definitely a day of New Hope. The screaming woman had been convinced that they were going to die out on the water. How unusual that they were adrift in the open ocean on a rare calm day with no wind or rolling ocean swell before we found them. Literally, *New Hope* entered their lives and convinced them that their prayers worked. New hope filled the crew's lives too, as the implementation of a simple creative idea onboard in the cleaning process made a significant change in the finished product coming out of the peeling machine, and helped to develop a new industry and new jobs.

I definitely believe in new hope for all.

New Hope

End of season, salmon are no more
Alaska has closed the worker's door
No more jobs in Alaska until next season
No salmon left to can, so that's the reason
Back home we go to what we don't know
Arriving home for a job I better start chasin'
Looking for a job in the town's boat basin
A production man I am and a fisherman, too
Any job I'll take even if it is to fill out a crew
Take what you can, even a tough job is okay
I'll take anything I can find, even if it's today
Just so ya know, I'll do anything, I'm no wimp
I'll even take a job working with shrimp.
Did I say shrimp? I must be outta my mind
No shrimp around here of any kind
I hate it when I'm wrong. Shrimp has been found
I got a job so I reckon I'll stick around
A machine peels off the shell pound after pound
I wanna see how they catch 'em, and I find a boat
It didn't take too long, I got on one named *New Hope*
Fishing thirty miles offshore, it is strange what one can see
We hear screaming out here, thirty miles at sea?
What could it be?

8
Overboard

I returned to my home in Westport on the Washington coast when my job ended in Ketchikan, Alaska. I needed to find work. A friend told me to go to the employment office and file a claim for unemployment.

I asked him, "How do you do that?"

"Just tell them something, and that there is no possible chance of getting work this time of year."

I thought that was a little strange, but I had never signed up for unemployment before so I figured I'd give it a try. So I went to the state employment agency in Aberdeen and filled out a form on my experience as a sign painter. After all, nobody paints signs in the winter in Grays Harbor County.

I figger'd I had it made. After two weeks with no work, I would get a check for $20.

The next day I received a call from a sign company that needed a name painted on a boat. I couldn't believe it!

So, being such a naïve, honest guy, I appeared at the sign company, and they showed me the boat. I was to paint the name on the port and starboard bow and the stern. It was a small troller. The troller's name was the *EDIZ*. I was happy the name wasn't longer, like *Penelope* or *Georgianna*.

Apparently, I did too good a job, because the painting outfit informed me that they would call when they had another job. No $20 unemployment check this time. However, I got paid $20 for painting the name of the boat.

The next job I applied for was as a steeplejack. Now, I knew there would be no calls for that job, because there were no steeples in Grays Harbor. After about two weeks, when I was thinking I was going to get a check, I instead received a call from the employment agency. They had a job for me at the Weyerhaeuser mill in Aberdeen. I ask what the job was. They told me the Weyerhaeuser smokestack was ready for new stainless-steel bands close to the top, to keep the bricks from separating. I told them I couldn't do it, because I had another job.

So much for my unemployment checks. I have never received an unemployment check in my life. I had decided it was just too much of a hassle. It was easier to get a job.

And that was how I went to work rigging crab gear for the upcoming Dungeness crab season.

Bill Nelson had been fishing in Alaska, and he was looking for a man to complete his crew for Washington's crab season opening in December. His boat was the *Tillie M.* My dad fished on this boat in the early 40s with Hubert Quiren, though the *Tillie M*'s name had nothing to do with our family name.

Charlie Norris, Bill Nelson, and I were rigging new crab pots and using manila line because polypropylene hadn't been invented yet. Bill Nelson had us splicing every connection. No knots. Just splices. Four splices to each pot and buoy. Fingers bleed after about 40 splices. We worked gear for about six weeks. Back in those days, if you wanted a job on a boat, you worked the gear for no pay. That was because you were going to make so much money fishing, it more than made up for all your hard work and time when you didn't get paid.

The day the season opened, the wind also opened. The Grays Harbor bar was not safely passable for small crab boats. The bar is an area where the deep waters of the Pacific Ocean meet the shallower waters near the mouth of the harbor. However, it didn't stop the big lumber-carrying ships from entering or leaving. We waited out the weather along with all the others, our decks loaded with Dungeness crab pots.

We finally steamed out of the harbor along with about 50 other crabbers. Chet Peterson's boat, the *Mylark*, was alongside us, heading north. We dropped our gear where no others were dropping theirs, laying out three strings of 30 pots. Then we headed back in to get more gear.

We managed to get all the crab pots out, by which time we were ready to check the first pots. We pulled up some snails and a starfish. Not a good sign. Had we dumped the gear on a rock pile?

Captain Nelson, I learned, had never fished off the west coast for crab before. Bringing up several more pots, we never got one crab. I mentioned to Chuck that was probably why there were no other boats anywhere near us.

Fortunately, Donna, my children's mother, was able to support the family with her job in a cannery.

Back on the *Tillie M*, things weren't going so well. We never seemed to place the pots where the crabs lived. We went out when few others ventured over the bar. Captain Nelson had determined that the *Tillie M* was part submarine, and we continued to fish in mountainous seas and cold, nasty weather. One time we were pulling gear in swells that appeared to be 10- to 15-footers, and at times we rolled so far over, the rails were scooping up water. I had hooked a crab pot buoy with the buoy hook that was attached to a 10-foot-long bamboo pole. We came up on a swell, and the buoy started to pull the hook out of my hands. Leaning over the rail, trying to get unhooked, instead of letting go, I was jerked overboard!

The water in January off the coast of Washington is not warm. I had on rain gear over my hip boots. We all wore hip boots back in those days—a big no-no. I surfaced holding onto my hip boots, using them as a flotation device. I had no clue how I had removed those boots underwater!

I frantically looked for the *Tillie M*. It had disappeared! Then I saw it turning around and rolling heavily in the swell. Then it was gone again!

I wondered if they saw me, because I had on dark green rain gear. I had hair back then, so I didn't have a shining bald head that would have been easier to see. The next thing I realized, the boat was so close I thought it would run right over me! As I had slipped into a trough, the *Tillie M* rolled in the swell right above me, and I thought I was done for! As I was coming up on the swell, the boat rolled the starboard rail over towards me, and Chuck reached out, grabbed hold of me, and pulled me out of the sea and threw me on the deck like a landed fish.

I felt like I had been dropped from the yardarm. I shivered from the cold and near drowning.

Chuck said, "Goddamnit, Jerry, we haven't finished the string yet! And I suppose you dropped my pliers."

Our hard-ass skipper decided to call it a day, so we rode the breakers over the bar and tied up in the harbor. There was a sort-of standard held by the fishermen, that if Chet Peterson on the *Mylark* didn't go fishing, no one went fishing.

The *Tillie M* had been built in a back yard in Westport in the 20s or early 30s. It had a high bow and the fo'c'sle (or forecastle) was below the bow. Inside the fo'c'sle was the crew's quarters, including a little stove just big enough to hold one small pot, like a two-quart pressure cooker, and a small sink. The aft bulkhead had a door into the engine room. Above deck sat a small wheelhouse, barely big enough for two people, along with the wheel, compass, throttle, and gear lever. No radars back in those days. Aft of the wheelhouse were two sliding doors—side by side. One door opened above the D13000 Caterpillar engine. The other door opened into a gear locker that held all our rain gear, and was just wide enough that one could stand in there with shoulders touching both sides, and roll with the boat without hanging onto anything. The door had a thick 10-inch square glass port about eyeball height. That gear locker was my hiding place when we were traveling.

Another incident aboard the *Tillie M* several days later caused me to seek other work. The skipper didn't appear to understand why no other boats had left the harbor except Chet Peterson's *Mylark*. Captain Peterson had left the harbor long before we did, heading north to get his gear. The sea was picking up as we started for our gear, swells too big to be fishing in.

You must realize that was my estimation, not the skipper's. We hauled gear regardless of the building seas. Finally, it was getting too rough to work safely, so we secured our gear, with some crab in the hold, and a few pots stacked on the stern.

The skipper turned the boat around and headed for the harbor entrance. Massive swells were generating some very large and ugly combers on the bar, but we were gonna head in regardless. We managed to ride a couple of big ones without broaching. Then we slipped down off a swell into the bottom of a more significant one building on our stern, which kept climbing higher and higher until I couldn't even see the top. As it started to break, and I slammed the gear locker door shut and thought, this is not going to lift us, it's going to bury us!

The wave broke and did bury the boat in green water, and it kept going down, and the water was squirting in around the door. There was no daylight out that window—just water! The exhaust was steaming off the engine as the water poured through cracks in the sliding door.

Then we rolled and surfaced into daylight. We took two more bad ones but never broached, and eventually made it in to tie up to the float. We lost all the pots tied off on the stern, and the hatch cover was gone, along with the crab. The spare lines we had tied on the railing atop of the wheelhouse left with the railing.

A couple of fishermen came down to the boat as I was tossing my sea bag on the dock and told us they had been watching us from the beach. They said we went down so far after that breaker hit us that the cross tree disappeared. They were sure that was the end of the *Tillie M*. Not this time, I thought.

I said goodbye to the skipper and Charlie Norris and left to find other work to hold me over until I could get back to Alaska. In three months I had made $500.

Overboard

Sometimes you just gotta do it, like it or not
Found a job on board a boat to fill an empty slot
The crab gear work is a tiring job for no pay
You do it waiting when we make the big payday
A job in the wet and cold is an easy task
How wet and cold, you ask?

9
Jerry's Luck, Good and Bad

I operated a cannery in Middle Bay, about 20 miles out of Kodiak past the Naval Air Station. My partner Harry Felton owned the building and the land on which it sat. I put the cannery together, and Harry supplied the necessary funds. We had a reasonable season freezing salmon for a Japanese buyer. Then we proceeded to install equipment for processing King crab. I was testing everything to determine if changes were required before production started.

The cooking tank was full, the water boiling vigorously. The whole elevated platform where the cooling and cooking tanks were located vibrated! Standing near the tank, I watched as the vibrations broke the welds on the platform's front bracing, causing it to collapse. The cooking tank tilted, boiling water covered the floor a foot deep, and the scalding liquid instantly filled both of my XtraTuf boots.

Indescribable pain filled my brain! I tore off boots and socks along with the first layer of skin, and then called Kodiak on the radio for someone to get me to the hospital. Driving my truck was totally out. By the time I arrived at the emergency room, my feet were swollen and grotesque. They had to cut my Levi's off. I thought, "To throw away a good pair of Levi's is also painful."

After several weeks of doctor visits, bandage changes, and crutches, I was ready to do something besides sitting around reading books and eating ice cream. My girth was starting to expand. I had no job, no income, and no prospects.

With a pair of loose-fitting boots on my feet, I set out looking for a job

My friend Doug Putansu owned and operated a boat named the *Kiska*. He had just returned to Kodiak from Adak, where he left the boat, to come home for Christmas. The *Kiska* was a wood-hull, house-forward King crabber. The boat had recently left the shipyard in Seattle where it had been painted and had two new Caterpillar engines and new piping installed. The engine room was rewired and had been painted white and it looked like an operating room. The *Kiska* was rigged for King crab fishing, but in those days, there was not a Marco KingHauler. We had a power block, but it lacked the power required to haul a full pot, so we had a chain driven capstan. We would take a few wraps around it to assist the power block. There was no deck crane or pot launcher. No line coiler. Everything was done by hand and a strong back. The *Kiska* was in Adak waiting for the King crab opening.

* * *

After the holidays, Doug called me about joining him for the King crab season. He said he needed a good cook and a deckhand, which came under "duties" in the job description. Two of the original crew had remained aboard, making four of us.

The boat was at anchor in Finger Bay on Adak Island. I didn't really want to go fishing, because my luck had been so bad. I didn't want to burden someone else with my problems. But my wife Donna was always on me to get a job, although I couldn't walk or stand up without crutches.

So I told Doug I really shouldn't go with him because with my luck the boat would catch fire, burn up, blow up, or sink.

"That's ridiculous," he laughed. "I need a cook, so pack your bag."

I gave it some thought, and it immediately dawned on me that I would be away from my nagging wife for about two months, make some fast money, and pay off some people who were kind enough to support me during my misfortune.

Things were looking up! Maybe my luck had changed!

Doug and I boarded the plane for Anchorage. An overnight in the big city waiting for the next flight to the Adak Naval Air Facility.

Adak Island lay about 1,200 miles west-southwest of Anchorage. It was December and 10 below zero in Anchorage. Hopefully, it would warm up considerably on arrival in Adak, which was famous for its weather and constant high-velocity winds—the windsock at the Naval Air Station was an anchor chain! Adak's other item of noted fame: there was a woman behind every tree. (Of course, there were no trees on Adak Island!)

Arriving in Adak at the Naval Air Facility we managed to get a ride to Finger Bay, located a few miles from the airstrip. We boarded the boat, and I met the crew. Freddie, the engineer, was quiet, round-faced, about 35, shorter than me; though heavy-set, he moved with youthful agility. The other deckhand, Maurice Page, I guessed to be around 40, a little graying around the temples. He was surly and seldom ever smiled. Rather, he just grouched around, and I got the impression that he didn't like me from the start. Maybe 'cause I got his job. That's a joke, because nobody wants to be cook on a fishing boat. Nonetheless, Maurice was always complaining about something, and my nickname for him was "Sorry Morry."

Now, one of the duties the cook was blessed with was procuring groceries. With no civilian, public store in Adak, the processing ships anchored in Finger Bay would order groceries from Seattle. The orders came in by air freight. Sometimes we could get groceries out of the processing ship's own stores, depending on its stock of supplies. Therefore, procuring groceries was a major operation, and often everything was at the discretion of the processing ship's head cook. Since I wasn't exactly a beginner in the processing business, I knew how things worked. I always made friends with the cook.

We stored the *Kiska*'s groceries on board the processing ship *Northgate*. The *Northgate* was a converted World War II liberty ship. Each vessel that delivered crab to the *Northgate* kept its locker in their enormous freezer hold. First thing, I went down into the frozen depths and located our locker. I retrieved enough groceries for about ten days. Fresh produce was just a figment of a boat cook's imagination. You could find a dinosaur egg in a snowbank easier than you could find a head of lettuce or a tomato.

We departed Adak on a rare calm day. The Bering Sea was flat and still, and I didn't get seasick. Seldom do I go to sea and manage to retain my last meal.

We fished our gear continuously for 36 hours without sleep, only stopping periodically to eat. I had to cook and work the deck at the same time, and Sorry Morry was a real joy to work with on deck. I got so irritated with him, I forget to upchuck my last meal. It seemed he slammed the pot door down on my fingers every time the opportunity presented itself. I finally hit him upside the head with a bait container that I had just removed from the pot—it had been down long enough for the bait to liquefy, and the smell would gag a maggot.

"Oops," I said. "Sorry, Morry, it must have slipped."

A couple more finger slams and some very stinking, ripe, slimy bait containers that had lost their way and ended up in his face finally calmed the fury of the beast.

Fishing along, minding our own business, all at once six huge sea lions came out of nowhere and tried to climb aboard the boat. They were barking and howlin' and crashing into the side of the boat trying to get over the rail. We stopped our fishing program to look for the reason for the sea lion invasion. No land in sight. We were miles from any rock or islet. The explanation became evident as soon as we spotted the killer whales circling our boat, just waiting for their breakfast. The orcas moved in for the kill, the sea lions frantic with nowhere to go. It wasn't long before the waters ran red. We weren't sad really. Sea lions eat their weight in fish every day or two. Alaska. Survival of the fittest.

We delivered our crab to the *Northgate*. It wasn't much for our first trip. I didn't make any big bucks.

Next day we got ready to set sail again for the fishing grounds. But we needed to restock groceries, especially onions. I talked to the cook, and he agreed to swap one of our cases of breakfast sweet rolls for a 25-pound bag of onions. It was like the catch of the day. I couldn't have been happier. Onions were a staple in the food I prepared and the crew devoured as if it was their last meal. I always washed my pots and pans as I used them, because no one else ever cleaned them after use, and then you couldn't get them clean even with a steam hose and sandpaper.

We departed the protected waters of Finger Bay into Sitkin Sound and turned east heading out south of the Aleutian Islands into the North Pacific. Hearing that some King crab had found their way around to the Pacific side of the Aleutians, we had moved some of our gear from the Bering Sea to an area south of Amlia Island.

As soon as we entered Asuksak Pass, the bow started to dive. It was not going to be a smooth sailing trip.

Rounding Cape Ruin on Umak Island, I then knew why it was called Cape Ruin. When it's blowing southeast at 50 knots, it just ruins your trip. The 60 miles to our gear was not going to be at our normal speed of 8 knots—we were lucky to make 5. The wind increased by the hour, screaming in the rigging, building ice!

Not long after dark the 50-knot winds had risen to 100, the sea turned into a raging maelstrom of 30-foot-high rollers and crashing waves. I wondered why I had taken the job. I knew it wasn't going to be a rowboat on a windless lake. It's amazing what one will do when you have no money. Now I remembered why I took those shore side jobs of operating canneries, designing production systems, and attacking underwater projects that required my skills as a working commercial diver. *Too late to be thinking about that.*

Skipper Doug Putansu decided to steer north and seek shelter in the lee shore of Atka Island. This island has many rock piles and little unknown spires that jut up from the depths surrounding it. Some weren't even on the charts. Fortunately, Doug has been fishing out here long enough to know the bays and inlets that afforded safe anchorage.

We were huddled in the wheelhouse, looking at the radar, and it all seemed rocks and death. White foaming water crashed into the window glass. We snaked our way around the rocks, maintaining steerage-way, trying for Kobakof Bay. We turned hard over, broadside into the 30-foot swells and rolled the rails under as the vessel slowly returned to a more or less even keel. The entrance to this hole in the rock wall was not possible! So we headed back out, away from the small rock-strewn coast. In these seas, Kobakof Bay was impossible! Waves crashed into the rocks with such force, the roar was heard inside the wheelhouse.

Somehow we made it around Sagchudak and Amtigas Islands right back into the full fury of the storm.

Our next try, Vasilief Bay.

It seemed to take an eternity! We made little headway. We climbed one monstrous wave, slid down the other side, climbed the next. Time dragged on like the hour-hand on a clock.

We finally made the point of land round to Vasilief Bay. Thank God for radar, or whoever invented it. We slipped through the narrow passage, out of the Pacific Ocean's screaming storm and violent savage seas.

Vasilief Bay was flat calm!

One other King crab boat lay at anchor in the bay. The *Kevleen K.*

It was 0200 hours. Two a.m. We dropped anchor, crashed exhausted into our bunks.

My bunk lay fore-and-aft right across the narrow passageway from the galley to the wheelhouse and across from the engine room door. We'd been crashed in our bunks maybe an hour when the smell of smoke woke me up. I rolled out and grabbed the engine room doorknob. The same moment, Doug's hand covered mine. We opened the engine room door together and were greeted by orange flames. We slammed the door.

"Fire in the engine room!" I hollered.

We plugged all the vents to the engine room with our sleeping bags. The engine room had a fixed CO_2 fire suppression system with an activator in the wheelhouse, which Doug hit, triggering the extinguisher.

Having been Kodiak Assistant Fire Chief for six years and a graduate of the Navy firefighting school at Kodiak Naval Air Station, I knew, in a fire situation, you never opened an engine room door until you were certain a fire was completely out. So, when I said we needed to wait, to my surprise everyone did as I told them, even Sorry Morry.

Doug decided we should get over to the *Kevleen K* to see if they would come alongside our boat and standby. We went up on top of the wheelhouse to get the aluminum skiff, which was full of buoys and line—what a big mess! After cleaning it out, we managed to get the skiff to the deck and over the rail into the water. No one noticed the 12-footer's keel had filled with rainwater and frozen, splitting its seams. Doug found the prehistoric Gale outboard, which I would have bet my earnings would never start. He and I boarded the skiff and attached the outboard to the stern.

I asked Doug, "We got any oars for this high-speed launch?"

He replied simply, "No."

The old outboard had a top fuel tank, which Doug filled. Then he wrapped the starting rope around the spindle and gave it one pull. I would have lost my earnings had I made the bet, because that prehistoric outboard roared to life!

We were about to untie the skiff when I noticed we were sinking. I hollered to Sorry Morry to fetch a bucket as I handed the bow line to Freddie, then secured the stern line to the *Kiska*'s rail. Balancing on the skiff's seat, I bailed enough until we could see why we were sinking. There was a three-foot-long crack in the keel. The seawater had thawed the ice and started to fill the boat again. Our luck was not improving.

There was no life raft on board. The little aluminum 12-footer with a cracked keel was all we had. I didn't have time to think about what would have happened if the fire had been worse and we were still out in heavy seas! Picture a sinking 12-foot aluminum boat on 20- to 30-foot seas and 100-knot winds. *Hello Davey Jones. Guardian angel, I hope you are here.*

We still weren't certain if the engine room fire was completely out. We needed another platform. It was that or the beach.

Braving the leaky skiff, me bailing and Doug steering, we motored over to the *Kevleen K*, about 100 yards away. Maurice and Freddie waited on the *Kiska*'s stern away from the house because the smoke was billowing out the galley door. The fire still burned. The CO_2 system had failed.

Doug and I pulled up alongside the *Kevleen K*, and I jumped aboard with two lines to tie the skiff off to the rail so it wouldn't sink. I stayed with the skiff, while Doug went into the galley through the deck door in search of the crew. Everyone was sound asleep. Who could blame them? A secluded bay on Atka Island at four in the morning?

Doug managed to get them up and they cranked up the main. Doug explained our dire situation. Soon the *Kevleen K* pulled up anchor and headed toward the *Kiska*.

They tied off by the stern, and I jumped to the *Kiska*'s aft deck.

I immediately ran into the galley, holding my breath, got to my bunk, slid the drawer out from under and grabbed a pair of long johns still in a cellophane wrapper. I reached in under the drawer and put my hand on the deck, which was right over the engine room. It was really hot! Not a good sign. I was almost overcome by smoke. I headed out the door and onto the deck.

Back up on deck, bent over, I breathed in fresh air.

No time. It was abandon ship.

We loaded the light-weight aluminum skiff aboard the *Kevleen K*, and she quickly backed away from the burning *Kiska*. None of us had time to grab clothes or personal gear. All I had was the one package of long johns. It was still 20 degrees.

As the *Kevleen K* backed, we all watched the flames burn through the hatchway leading up to the wheelhouse like a firebomb had gone off. It blew the windows out of the wheelhouse, and the upper deck became a raging inferno. We all stared in disbelief at the sight of our boat on fire. As it burned down to the waterline, the fuel tanks erupted into a massive ball of yellow fire, thus ending the life of the *Kiska* as it sank silently below the surface of the bay.

Along with the loss of the *Kiska* was my recently acquired 25-pound sack of onions. Well, besides all lost clothes, personal belongings, and other gear. We had escaped with the clothes on our backs.

I opened the package of long johns I had salvaged from under my bunk. As I tried to remove them, they crumbled in my hands from the heat.

If the *Kevleen K* had not been in that bay that night, we would have had to make it to the beach—where there was no shelter or even wood for a fire. It wouldn't have been long before we'd have frozen to death. No one would have known where we were or what had happened to the *Kiska* and her crew.

The *Kevleen K*'s crew took good care of us, giving us warm shelter, food, coffee. They saved our lives. We waited out the storm in the protection of Vasilief Bay. Then the *Kevleen* K sailed straight for Adak Naval Air Station, where we parted with the crew with grateful thanks.

From there we went to the terminal to catch a Reeve Aleutian Airways flight back to Anchorage, and then on to Kodiak. On arrival at the Adak terminal, it became evident that none of us had any money or identification. Back in those days, they had National

Bank of Alaska counter checks. You could fill out a counter check for any amount, within reason of course, and take care of a purchase. Alaskans did it all the time. So, I grabbed a blank check payable to Reeve Aleutian Airways, put in the amount required to get us a flight back to Kodiak. I think it was just under a thousand dollars.

I tried to call home to tell my wife what had happened, and that I was on my way home, but there was no answer. We all boarded the plane, still attired in our boat clothes smelling of crab juice, squid bait, smoke, and body odor. We had no choice, lucky just to be alive. We were used to the smell, but our fellow passengers looked at us with wrinkled noses and tried in vain to separate themselves from our presence. We didn't bother telling any of them the circumstances of our appearance.

On arrival in Anchorage, I called Bob Reeve, owner of Reeve Aleutian Airways, and told him that I had just written a check at his terminal in Adak, and there was no money to cover the amount. I explained what had happened and why we had no money. Bob was a good friend, and we belonged to the same organization, the Navy League of the United States, and I just happened to be the president. He told me not to worry about it. I could pay him whenever it was convenient.

In Kodiak, Doug's wife was there to meet him. There was no one to meet me, but that was not a surprise. Doug dropped me off on his way home. I opened the front door and stepped inside to an empty house. Somehow, she missed a fork in a drawer in the kitchen. Other than that, she'd left the kitchen cabinets, toilet, sink, and tub. I think if she could have taken those too, she would have. I looked in the closet to see if she'd taken my clothes as well. On the closet floor lay a big pile of my stuff. She hadn't answered my phone call, because the phone was also missing. At least she'd left my diving gear that was in the garage and, happily, my trusty '67 Chevrolet truck. I jumped in and drove downtown to Solly's Bar and Restaurant. I borrowed a couple hundred dollars from Martin Urie, the owner, to tide me over and get a meal. I was starving. My money and wallet were somewhere at the bottom of Vasilief Bay. The next day I had to arrange for another driver's license and necessary identification cards.

Donna had run off with Kodiak Airway's helicopter pilot, Ron Mosgood. It was time to celebrate, and I did just that.

I had to have a job, so I convinced the manager of Pacific Northern Airways in Kodiak, another close friend, to get me on a plane to Seattle. (He and his son had saved my life a few years before by getting me to a hospital when I had spinal meningitis.)

Arriving in Seattle, I was immediately hired to manage all of Northern Seafoods' processing facilities in and around Kodiak Island.

Before heading north, I went shopping and found the largest, most significant "Thank You" card. It was about a foot long. I addressed it to Ron Mosgood. On the bottom I wrote, "You are the best friend I ever had."

Jerry's Luck

My luck was finally changing for the better.
There are no onions, lettuce, or eggs in the shell
Adak Island has no garden or groceries to sell
Fresh anything way out here is a no, no, no
It's easier to find a dinosaur egg in a bank of snow
Beg and plead just for a few onions in a sack
I got onions at a high cost and I ain't lookin' back

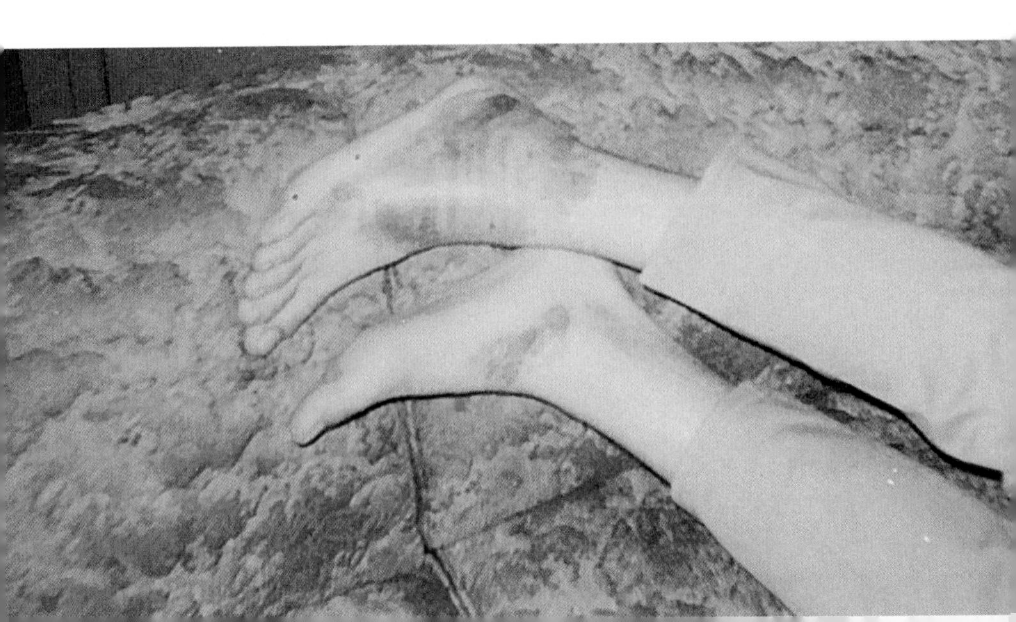

10
Tsunami

On March 25, 1964, our 75-foot wooden shrimp boat, the *Fortress*, arrived in Kodiak at Eastpoint Seafoods' processing facility dock to offload 100,000 pounds of shrimp. That may sound like a big pay-day, but the price was only 3 cents per pound. The *Fortress*' crew consisted of the captain, Ted Moseley, whom we called Skipper, the cook, Buck Lorton, myself as engineer, and our new deckhand and web repair expert, George Horn. Horn came aboard to replace Oral Burch. Oral's brother Al Burch had called from Seward that their boat, the *Celtic*, was out of the shipyard and ready to go fishing. (The *Celtic* rode that tsunami up into the trees somewhere in Seward; it never made it to the water again.)

Kodiak Island lies in the Gulf of Alaska, 58 degrees north and 152 degrees west. Approximately 250 miles southwest of Anchorage, Alaska, the city of Kodiak is located on a narrow bench of coast at the northeast tip of the island. Mountains rise abruptly behind slopes northeast to southwest down to the island-studded St. Paul Harbor. Twenty miles southeast of the harbor is Cape Chiniak, the easternmost point of the island. The Kodiak boat harbor is in the northernmost point of St. Paul Harbor and surrounded by a man-made rock breakwater. Most of St. Paul Harbor is unprotected to the southeast and open to the Gulf of Alaska.

In 1964, several canneries and other fishery-related businesses were located on the shore of the harbor and the channel, between Kodiak Island and Near Island. Situated in the channel was Kodiak Electric's generating plant. The distance between the two islands at one point was about 50 yards. From the boat harbor entrance across the Near Island Channel lay a very small indentation in the rock shoreline named Dog Bay. I don't know why it was called Dog Bay—maybe someone lost their dog there. The depth of the channel was relatively consistent at about 10 fathoms, and the shore-side facilities were attached to the shore with their docks constructed far enough into the channel to accommodate the fishing and freight vessels. All the docks were about 6 feet above normal high water. The Kodiak city dock was a third of a mile southwest of the boat harbor and received all of the town's freight. Most of the structures were built on pilings jutting out into St. Paul Harbor. The city warehouse was located there, along with Kodiak King Crab Company, Eastpoint Seafoods, and Alaska Cold Storage. The next dock, about a 100 feet southwest, was the Union Oil dock. Gibson Cove lay a mile southwest of the Union Oil dock, and the Navy base 4 miles southwest of the Kodiak boat harbor.

Early morning of the 27th, Good Friday, after the shrimp were off-loaded, we cleaned up the *Fortress* and moved her under the ice chute to take on ice for the next trip. We helped Oral get his gear off the boat and to the airport to catch a flight to Seward.

Back aboard the *Fortress*, we had to wait until after 5:00 in the afternoon when the tide would be low enough to allow the ice to gravity feed down the chute into the boat's fish hold.

The weather was unbelievably beautiful for Kodiak for this time of year—about 30 degrees, no wind, and just a few scattered clouds.

I drove to my house on Potato Patch Lake, about 2 miles out on Mission Road, and completed the installation of the new washer and dryer that I had just purchased the day before. I removed all my clothes and bedding from the boat to wash them. I put on clean clothes, a pair of Levi's, a flannel shirt, my wool socks, and XtraTuf rubber boots. My Navy surplus jacket in hand, I hurried out the door and back to the *Fortress* to help with the icing. I planned to return later to finish the laundry. While the rest of the crew lived aboard, I was the only certified Kodiak resident.

Almost supper time, I didn't want to miss out on anything our cook prepared, which fortunately for us was always great! The menu that evening was fresh halibut cheeks, macaroni salad, fried spuds and onions, plus fresh baked biscuits. When the boat ain't

pitchin' and jumping up and down, the cook took advantage of the calm and outperformed the norm.

I asked Buck, "Hey, where did you get the recipe for this epicurean delight?"

He just shrugged and replied, "It came off the back of a cement sack."

Always praise the cook regardless of what's being prepared, because one complaint and you were automatically the cook forevermore. The cook and the skipper never have to do the dishes, so it was up to the other two crewmen to perform that task; anything other than cook!

When I came aboard looking for a job, the skipper asked me if I could cook.

"Sure I can cook," I replied. I was desperate.

He came back with, "Sorry, we already have a cook." He then asked, "Can you mend net?"

I said, "If I have to, but I'm not very good at it."

Third time was the charm. There was only one job left, and I was going for broke. Ted said, "We already have a net man. How are you at engineering?"

I gave my standard reply, "No problem." Though I really hated mending one-inch mesh net with frozen fingers.

He then said, "Okay, jump aboard."

Supper wasn't quite done, so we went about our chores making ready for a midnight departure. I went down the ladder to the engine room about 5:30 and started the main to let it warm up. It was easier while it's running to oil the rocker arms of the 4-cylinder 150-horsepower Atlas slow-speed diesel, which practically filled the engine room. The front of the engine had a 5-foot diameter flywheel that weighed maybe half a ton, and once turning you had better stay clear. The engine produced a sound like "ka-chug, ka-chug, ka-chug"—not like today's diesel engines that purr like a tranquil kitten. I went forward to the bank of batteries and started to fill them with water as needed.

As I was pouring water into the battery cells from a small can, the boat started to vibrate. It was rapidly moving up and down, not sideways as if another boat was passing by. Unlike anything I had ever experienced, it got so violent that I couldn't hold on to the can or the batteries. I looked back at the engine thinking the flywheel was coming off or the engine was out of control and ready to leave the engine room. Once I had convinced myself that this was not the case, I made my way past that monster flywheel up the ladder and onto the shaking deck.

I looked up under the dock. It rolled like waves on water, its shims falling out from under the planks. A ripping sound filled the evening as the big spikes were pulled out of the planks by the dock's undulation. Light poles danced with such intensity, I was certain they would snap, and electrical wires whipped up and down with such force they sang with a swishing sound.

The *Fortress* was shaking so much, we could hardly stand up without holding on to something. It was obvious we were having a massive earthquake that didn't seem to want to stop quakin' and shakin'!

Back in 1949, in a courthouse in Montesano, Washington, I'd experienced an earthquake, lasted maybe a minute. Seemed to me this one lasted more like four or five!

In those moments, from the boat deck, we watched in disbelief as the rock breakwater sank before our eyes, It turned out the island dropped over five feet! Then at the same time, the bottom under the dock where all cannery waste had accumulated for years roiled to the surface and brought some nose-hair-removing and eye-burning odors with it.

A very big, husky young man was in the ice house that was built on top of the cannery roof. It was swaying with such violence we were surprised that it stayed up there. When the shaking and swaying stopped he came out of that small crawl-through door like he had been shot out of a cannon. He hit the deck running, and all you could see was his rear end going up the hill kicking up gravel.

Jim Major came out on the dock and was going to move my truck to safe ground, but couldn't get it started. It was an old Navy surplus panel truck that I used to carry my diving gear. There was no ignition key to the truck because I used a knife switch under the steering wheel to start the truck and Jim didn't know that. I told Jim, "Forget about it. Get out of here! Don't worry about the truck. It'll be okay." I was always the incessant optimist.

We began to collect our senses and snap out of our earthquake-induced stupor. First thing I did was look for the fire ax to chop the lines off the cleats. I yelled to the skipper, "We gotta get away from the dock now! There's sure to be a tidal wave."

I axed our mooring lines. The main engine was running, so Skipper threw it in gear and pulled away from the dock and into the middle of the channel about 100 yards off. We drifted in front of the cold storage on the city dock and the Union Oil dock.

In just a few minutes, the water started receding like some unknown force had pulled a gigantic plug. Shocking and unbelievable event number two of the evening!

The water level continued to drop until we could see the bottom near the city dock—it dropped at least 25 feet in a matter of minutes.

"Where did the water go?" someone asked. Someone else, strangely calm, followed-up with, "And when do you think it's coming back?"

The vessel *Anna A* was sitting on the soft mud bottom in front of the city dock, and Norm Holm's King crab vessel *Neptune* had snapped her lines and was laying, wheelhouse seaward, on her side on the bottom between the Union Oil dock and the Cold Storage dock. Amazingly, all the King crab pots were still secured to her deck. We could see that Arne Hansen had the *Sea Quail* out in the channel, as did Dal Valentine on his boat, the *Rosemary*.

It was getting too dark to see into the harbor anymore. We were too far out. But I imagined that most of the boats were sitting on the bottom, maybe over a hundred of them, stranded there like dead whales.

The temperature dropped a little, no wind, and the surface of the water lay as flat as a pool table. In the galley our supper sat untouched. The four of us climbed the ladder to the flying bridge, atop the wheelhouse. It had identical controls, with better visibility for sliding into tight moorings. From there we had a little better view of the disaster that continued to unfold around us. Marine radios and CBs were alive with chatter.

I said to no one in particular that we better get ready for the wild rush of returning water coming back to fill this gigantic hole. None of us had on a watch, because when you work with nets on a rolling deck you don't wear anything that could catch on the web. Maybe half an hour went by, when we heard over the radio that a 50-foot tidal wave just hit Cape Chiniak. We made an immediate and unanimous decision to head into the wave thinking we had a better chance of survival.

Of course, we had no idea where the earthquake epicenter was or from which direction the wave was coming, but thought being out in the open area of St. Paul Harbor rather than in the channel or the confines of the inner harbor would be the best move at the time. I had this vision in my head of our little 75-foot boat climbing the vertical wave, and its breaking just before we reached the crest.

Heading southwest toward the Navy base, we were all keeping watch for the white foam teeth of this monstrous wave coming at us at hundreds of miles an hour. When we were adjacent to Gibson Cove, approximately one mile southwest of the city dock, the *Fortress* started to rise on a very large swell. She was running bow-up at a 20-degree angle and being carried backward towards the town. Skipper pushed the throttle full forward, but we were still going backwards. Ted told me to go below and drive a wedge in the throttle on the engine. I jumped to the deck and shot down into the engine room without touching one rung of the ladder. The main only turns about 300 RPM, but when I drove that wedge under the control lever it cranked up to 400 RPM—way over its design. I rushed back up to the flying bridge, not wanting to be in the engine room when the boat rolled over or sank.

The additional revolutions on the main engine must have helped, because we broke over the top of the swell and stared down into the second floor of the cold storage building. I saw my truck lifted up off the dock and disappear beneath the surface. I guessed it wasn't very watertight.

Even above the roar of the main engine, we could hear the wave tearing the town apart.

Once the skipper had determined we were in the clear, he sent me below again to pull the wedge from the throttle. No sooner was I out of the engine room, than the wave stormed into the harbor. The *Neptune*, which had been lying on its starboard side on the bottom, snapped to an upright position and floated wildly between the two docks. The skipper edged the *Fortress* in close enough that I could jump aboard and tie on a tow line to pull her out of what we considered a very dangerous place. We managed to get her alongside and made her fast to the *Fortress*.

After things calmed down a bit, with the *Neptune* still secured to us, we proceeded to round up small boats floating about aimlessly. Most of these boats were beach seiners that had been stored for the winter on huge racks alongside the cannery. We salvaged 13 of the boats and tied them off to pilings near the King Crab Cannery dock.

One of the largest King crab vessels in the area was the *Chief*, about 150 feet in length. It was secured to several pilings north of the city dock. There was no indication that it ever moved other than up and down with the variations of water levels, therefore we secured the small boats beside it.

The city, what was left of it, had gone completely dark. We did not have big flood lights on the *Fortress*, just deck lights, as we never fished after dark. One of the boats cruising around trying to stay out of trouble had a large searchlight flashing fore and aft; but it was no advantage to us.

We had just moved out into the harbor when the second wave roared in through the Near Island channel from the northeast and into St. Paul Harbor from the southwest. As the wave from the northeast came smashing through the narrow channel, it brought with it the fuel dock and fueling floats with all the fueling reels attached. Alaska Packers cannery went past us at about 20 knots, and I thought I saw an airplane but couldn't be certain. It appeared that Sutliff's entire stockpile from his lumber yard, some still bundled, was moving past, along with everything else that floated.

Trying to lasso another boat near the nonexistent entrance of the boat harbor, the northeastern wave hit us and drove us sideways into the southwestern wave. The combination of the two forces generated a giant whirlpool dragging us backwards at a 10-degree list into the swirling vortex—despite our main engine in full forward position. Skipper had the wheel hard over to no avail and yelled at me to go down and drive that wedge back into the throttle.

A red house on the hill just north of the city dock had been washed from its foundation and floated along with all the other flotsam, only this house had somehow managed to enter the swirling vortex inside of the *Fortress*. It started to break up and disappeared right before our eyes. We all stared right down into this black hole. A large knot formed in my stomach—I think this condition is known as fear. Being a fearless individual, I had never encountered anything of this magnitude.

Floats from the boat harbor were on the outer edges of the whirl-

pool, and one of them hit the *Chief.* One of the floats shot out and rammed the *Fortress* violently, rolling us hard over enough to barely escape the clutches of the swirling current. The float broke a couple planks and cracked a rib, though we didn't know it at the time.

The main engine exhaust pipe was red hot and blowing sparks and flame three feet out, not a good sign. Out of immediate danger from the whirlpool, I went back down to the engine room and removed the wedge. I was pleasantly surprised that the engine wasn't on fire, it must have been 130 degrees in the engine room, and the old main was hot and smokin'. I oiled the rocker arms and checked 'er out before returning to the deck. I didn't want the old girl to quit on us now.

The skipper said, "I think we better get back out in the middle and forget about all the other boats and concentrate on saving our-

Above: View of Kodiak before the earthquake and tsumani. Below: Wreckage of boats in Kodiak harbor. At right: Mangled boats and destroyed buildings in the harbor.

selves." We had no problem with that decision, and set about avoiding all the debris in the water.

Not knowing what was happening in town, from the conversations on the radio we learned that about half the boats from the boat harbor were plugging up the streets. We witnessed some of the vessels going over the breakwater and some grounding on the rocks. The first wave evidently carried some boats from the harbor to new locations uptown, and the second wave removed some and took others farther uptown!

We headed out to the middle of the inner harbor and managed to grab another small boat and took it over to the pilings where we had secured the others.

We heard Bill Cuthbert answering someone on the radio when they asked his location. Bill said he wasn't sure but; thought he was up by the old school house; he had tied his boat, the *Selief*, to a telephone pole. We knew he had a load of live King crab aboard that he was supposed to unload. The crab would be getting very thirsty by now. They eventually unloaded the very dead King crab into a dump truck and hauled it away.

It was evident that the town of Kodiak had been devastated. We could see some of the buildings out in the harbor. The boat harbor was gone. Some of the floats out in the bay still held, two small boats were tied to one of them.

About this time another wave came in, and some of the boats that were up town, like the *Henning-J*, came back out and disappeared completely in a matter of minutes. Three days later, the *Henning-J* was found on the rocks on Holiday Island—a total loss.

Then some connection of the cold storage's ammonia system

must have broken loose, because anhydrous ammonia saturated the air. With no wind to blow it away, it just hung over the water, and was so strong we could hardly see and breathing became difficult. We had tears dripping from our cheeks and we tried to get down close to the deck, but that didn't help us breathe. I went into the engine room. Buck and George went into the galley and I don't know where the skipper was looking for breathable air. We steamed farther out in the harbor from the cold storage building. The air finally became more tolerable.

With no lights from the town, the night had become pitch black—other than a few of the surviving crewed vessels with lights, running around looking for survivors or anything else worth the effort to salvage.

Then I heard this voice from the water hollering, "Hey, Jerry! Jerry! Over here!"

I called up to the skipper to stop the engine. Someone was out there.

Again, "Jerry, over here! Wait! Wait!"

Recognizing the voice, I yelled, "Al, that you?"

Allen Vincent came into view of our deck lights, alone in a small punt that couldn't have been more than 6 feet long. He was on his knees paddling this wood chip of a boat with a little piece of wood about 3 feet long.

I threw him a line and pulled him alongside. He climbed aboard, got down on his hands and knees and kissed the deck several times.

We asked where he had been.

He said, "I was in the boat harbor when the shaking started. I was trying find out what was going on when floats started groaning and sinking. The next thing I know, water was rising and this little punt came flying by and I grabbed it and jumped in. Have been up town twice and back out, up the channel, down the channel, over to Near Island. I think at one time I was about to the Navy base. I rode that last wave back here."

Wet, cold, and shaking, he told us of a lot of screaming and crashing buildings and hanging on for dear life. His eyes shone red in the deck lights, and he complained about the ammonia-saturated air.

We got him into the galley where it was warm. Our dinner was still untouched, sitting on the table.

We continued drifting about, the big *Neptune* still tied alongside, trying to figure out what to do next. No one had a clue when or if the next wave was coming. Seemed that we had one running about every 45 minutes all night long!

Despite everything else, the weather favored us. The stars shone bright as only they do in Alaska's seas, with no big city lights and air pollution—except for the lingering smell of ammonia still leaking out of the cold storage. Wind speed was zero, the temperature hovering just below freezing. There was so much going on minute to minute that we had no time to think about anything other than saving the boat and ourselves, and doing anything else we could to help in this devastation.

At last, daylight started to creep up over the chaos of the night, and our relief was beyond imagining. Not that we thought it was over! It was just that your mind and body seem to function better when you can see. We decided it was safe to move in toward the city dock, and if it was still intact, we might find moorings for the *Neptune*, which was still tied up to us.

Approaching the dock, it appeared to be stable, though lots of planks were dislodged and its surface was totally bare. Not a single pallet, crate, or vehicle remained to mar the cleansing of the deck performed by Mother Nature. Amazingly, dock buildings appeared to be intact. We tied the *Neptune* off with plenty of slack and moved back into the channel to wait for more daylight—and maybe another wave.

The sky now brightened enough to see, and what a sight to behold! The bay was full of battered boats, harbor floats, lumber, and building roofs—some with the rest of the building still attached beneath. Oil covered the flat surface of the water in an eerie still life of destruction. The rock breakwater for the boat harbor had boats hanging off of it and perched on top of it and laying alongside it.

Uptown, boats were everywhere, the 80-foot *Hekla* appeared to be perched on top of the bowling alley. Our radio crackled continuously with calls for those missing by those looking for them. Arne Hansen on the *Sea Quail* gave reports to Dottie Valen of the Alaska Communications System on the locations of miscellaneous boats.

The *Kingfisher* floated in Dog Bay as if nothing had happened. She didn't seem to show any damage whatsoever. During the night's turmoil Arne Hansen on the *Sea Quail* had grabbed it as it was going by and towed it over there and released the anchor. He wasn't aware that the owner, Fritz Deveau, a crab fisherman and the mayor's brother, was asleep on board. Passed out would be more accurate because dropping an anchor right over your head should wake up the soundest of sleepers. The story went: Fritz got up the next morning, walked out on deck, looked over at the location of the boat harbor, saw there was no boat harbor, saw some boats laying on their sides in the streets and the unbelievable mess of what was once a town, and crawled back into his bunk thinking he was having a nightmare.

Our dauntless *Fortress* was still floating, her old Atlas engine still churning away at the sea astern, seemingly none the worse from the previous night's high-speed, fire-belching show.

Broad daylight filled the sky above, and people started to move around, checking out the damage. And there was a lot of damage to check out. It had been a catastrophic night. Most of Kodiak's downtown buildings were gone!

We tied up to the city dock, not knowing what to do next, when Charlie Warner, a friend of mine, came down the dock to our boat. He had been staying at my house while working on the construction of the newly rebuilt cold storage, and had spent the night up on Pillar Mountain, over a thousand feet high overlooking the town.

I got off the boat, and the two of us made our way down the broken plank dock over to the cold storage to survey the damage. Just as we got inside, a tremendous aftershock just about knocked us down. Our exit was immediate. We got in Charley's truck and managed to get partway to my house by driving over and around whatever was in the roadway. We had to walk about a mile the rest of the way. Coming up over the hill where the Beachcombers nightclub had been only the day before, we continued on to where my house was just to the right and in back of the Beachcombers on Potato Patch Lake.

Before us everything had changed, and we stared in stunned silence! No Beachcombers. No Potato Patch Lake. And no sign of a house where Jerry Tilley once lived. We walked over to the location of the house and found a pipe wrench. That was it. Even the concrete foundation blocks and what little grass I once had were gone.

Potato Patch Lake was a shallow lagoon. I had the clothes on my back, nothing else. It had all gone out to sea.

Three paintings of my kids were my most significant loss—Dorothy Louise, Kathleen Ann, and "Corky" Jerry Jr. The house and all the material things I owned were gone. But that loss could not compare to loss of the three oil paintings I had mounted on the wall in my living room. These pictures were all I had to remind me of what I cherished the most in life, my family. And now they too were gone!

My dog Wolf, a McKenzie River Husky mix, was also nowhere to be found. I called and called for him. Charley and I searched around the area to finally find Wolf up in a tree. He had a bone sticking out of his back and couldn't walk, but he was sure tail-wagging happy to see me. With a neighbor's tender love and care he did survive.

Amid all the destruction and loss, there was one thing I was thankful for—besides finding Wolf alive. I had loaned all my diving gear to Jack Woosley, who lived up on the hill away from the sea. And there you have it, Jerry Tilley ended up with some diving gear but no house, no clothes, no bedding, no truck, and no money.

One strange occurrence after the tsunami. The water level in the bay didn't appear to change but a few inches for days. The sea had become still as a lake. There were no tides. I never heard an explanation for this strange phenomenon. Even some of the scientists that arrived soon after couldn't explain it. Several days later, the tides resumed. Nature took up her familiar routine.

As details of damage to other villages and communities rolled in, it was determined that we had lived through an earthquake of a magnitude never before recorded in North America, eventually set as 9.2 on the Richter scale. Some of us heard on the radio, from down in the lower 48, newscasters claiming Kodiak Island had sunk into the sea. It did sink, but not completely.

Until Saturday morning, the 28th of March, many in Kodiak didn't know the extent of the damage nor the details about the earthquake and tsunami. Near Island Channel was totally clean, Kodiak Airways floats and all the planes were gone. The shipyard was gone. Standard Oil dock and fueling floats were gone. Alaska Packers cannery and dock were gone. And the big hardware and marine supply store was also gone. A few pilings were left standing in the Near Island Channel, but other than that nothing remained. The channel choked down to about 50 yards wide in one spot, so I could imagine that wave from the northeast squeezing down in that narrow spot, and the force coming out the southwest end of the channel right where we were when it hit us. We hadn't been able to see it coming, but we certainly knew what it was when it hit us!

That quiet Saturday morning, Charlie and I returned to the boat after surveying the damage in the city and the area where my house had stood. We stepped aboard to have a cup of coffee. The meal from the evening before was still on the table stone cold, like a memorial to the night before. Ted, Buck, and George sat at the galley table drinking coffee, all in apparently delayed shock.

One of the newer 80-foot steel King crab vessels, the *Jaguar*, according to a witness, went down that channel northward end over end, to finally settle to the sea bottom in 85 feet of water between Woody Island and Kodiak Island. (This boat was raised several years later by two divers, Bill McLinn and me. It was purchased by Fred and Ruth Brechan and renamed the *Walter N.*)

The official Kodiak City report of April 6, 1964, listed 35 boats sunk or aground, 17 missing, 25 with significant or considerable damage, and 20 with slight damage. The epicenter of the earthquake was about 300 miles northeast of Kodiak Island in Prince William Sound, very close to Valdez, Alaska. The first wave hit Kodiak about 30 minutes after the earthquake, traveling at 600 miles per hour. From the epicenter of the quake, it was a straight shot out of Prince William Sound southwest to Kodiak Island for the numerous tsunami waves it generated. Unfortunately, the damage to outlying Kodiak Island villages was extremely severe.

Kodiak's downtown area was virtually destroyed. The bars must have lost their doors because the town was littered with thousands of bottles of booze, cases of it! Word was issued to all, "Do not drink the booze, it may be contaminated." So all the people I knew and some I didn't volunteered to test every bottle they could find. It was later determined that all the unopened bottles were free of contamination. (No one believed that contaminated statement for a minute.)

There were no telephone communications to the outside world until some telephone people managed to get the system working early Saturday morning. In the meantime, local ham operators were in contact with others on the mainland and got the word out that Kodiak Island had not sunk into the sea. In the first seven days after the disaster the emergency communication's system handled about 3,000 telegrams.

Thanks to the U.S. Navy, they airlifted about 300 homeless people to the lower 48 states and loaned the city some emergency generators. Within a couple days, power was restored to some of the town.

The city discussed the possibility of urban renewal in the near future. The town had needed some upgrading and repair, but not performed by Mother Nature! We were not ready.

Footnote: Ben Gerke was my insurance agent. That Friday morning, before the great earthquake, and after purchasing my new washer and dryer, I paid Ben a visit and raised the insurance on my house and contents. I paid him $43 for the additional premium. Fortunately, his office was not destroyed, and he was there the next Monday morning when I walked in and revealed my sad story that my house had burned down. He exclaimed with wide eyes and obvious shock, "Really. When did that happen?" I answered, "About 10 minutes before the wave washed all the ashes out to sea." He looked at me, smiled and reached in a drawer, sorted through some papers, and handed me my $43 check. Then he said, "I'm really sorry Jerry, but you didn't have tidal wave insurance." I said, "This I already know, why did you think I told you it burned down?" I did have full coverage fire insurance. It just wasn't my day.

Tsunami

A nice day to unload our shrimp load because it was a lot
I take all my bedding and my clothes to a washer I just bought
Load them in the washer and some washed ones in the dryer, too
I head back to the boat to help clean up deck and gear with the crew
The shaking started severely then it got worse and hard to stand
Over the radio came a notice of a fifty-foot wave heading for land
Heading for the sea, not land, we are safe right here you and me

11
Boat Secrets

On March 8, 1968, the Soviet submarine *K-129* sank in the North Pacific, no clue as to why. It was a top-secret submarine carrying nuclear missiles. However, the CIA—sneaky devils that they are—knew about it. They also knew that it had gone down somewhere between Alaska and the Hawaiian Islands. They had determined that it was worth finding and raising to collect the intact nuclear missiles and codebooks. In 1970, they began Project Azorian, one of the most complex, expensive, and secret intelligence operations of the Cold War, at a cost of $800 million (4 billion in today's dollars).

The Soviet Union was unable to locate *K-129*, but the U.S. knew where to look based on data recorded by four AFTAC sites and Adak, known as SOSUS, a hydrophone network in the North Pacific, which had identified an acoustic event on March 8 that likely originated from an explosion aboard the submarine. The U.S. zeroed in the location within 5 miles. The submarine USS *Halibut* from the Hawaiian Islands was ordered to the area. It had the capability to tow a submersible "fish," a 12-foot long, 2-ton unit that had a collection of cameras, strobe lights, and sonar, and could withstand extreme depths.

Now the U.S. had to build something that could reach the estimated depth and somehow lift that submarine to the surface. The yard that built the *Glomar Challenger* in 1968 was the obvious one to replicate that ship's capabilities. The *Glomar Challenger* was 400-foot deep-sea research and scientific drilling platform ship.

The company contracted to build the ship for the Navy was

owned by Howard Hughes, who was already working with the CIA on other classified operations. The ship was built and financed by Hughes and named the *Hughes Glomar Explorer*. The vessel used a cover story to convince the public that they were going to mine manganese nodules on the seafloor.

Back in the 1960s, living in Kodiak, Alaska, I had joined a group of oceanographers known as Oceanus and located in Miami, Florida. I got the latest developments on the ocean's activities and the newest information on miscellaneous fish species, etc. It came by mail in the form of a magazine, though sometimes just a flyer for the latest news.

I read an article in one of those leaflets about a vessel being built which would be able to drill into the earth's surface in order to check on the composition of the sediment of the seafloor 14,000 feet below. A 140-foot tower like an oil derrick rose up from the middle of the ship. This ship could also determine the drift in the Atlantic trench that separated the continents and running from the southern tip of South America up and through the middle of Iceland. The *Oceanus* article about the building of this ship to mine manganese from the seafloor gave the date it was to depart the shipyard and head out to sea. I was more than a little interested in this project.

At the time, I was president of the Navy League in Kodiak, Alaska. I was close to naval operations located in Kodiak and Adak, as I had accompanied the admiral on many trips to the Adak Naval Air Station and submarine base. I was in meetings, some of which were not informational to my ears, except for one conversation that mentioned the lost submarine I had remembered about when I lived in Kodiak.

Here are some details of the ship that secretly held steady over that sunken Soviet submarine, south of the Aleutian chain. It was built like the *Glomar Challenger* with a 140-foot derrick midship. It used oil drilling pipe in 30-foot sections that were threaded and screwed into the receiving pipe, thus making a long flexible drilling pipe that could be used to hold a huge grappling device to attach to the submarine and bring it to the surface from several thousand feet below. You must understand that this was a top-secret, clandestine operation known only to a select group and the CIA.

One day, I received a phone call from a guy who asked me if I knew anyone with a vessel that could carry a few tons of pipe to a location south of the Aleutian Islands. They would fly it to Dutch Harbor and load it on the boat for delivery to a designated location. I told him I was certain I could find one of our King crab vessels that would agree to it, if they could be paid a substantial amount to compensate for lost fishing time. He agreed to whatever it would cost. I asked, "Will this boat be going out to the *Glomar*?" He gasped, hesitated, then said, "What did you say?" I repeated that question. He wanted to know what I knew and where I got my information. I told him I thought everybody knew what was going on out there.

The next day two guys arrived by private jet in Dutch Harbor and asked the airport manager where they could find Jerry Tilley.

My friend called me on the radio and told me two guys were coming to the ship to see me, and they must be important government types, because they were wearing suits.

At that time, neither I nor they knew that part of the submarine had already been raised to the surface—though the grappling device had failed and part of the sub sank back to the bottom. They did recover two missiles and the bodies of six Russian sailors.

The guys approached my ship, the *Vita*. I came ashore to meet them. They introduced themselves and showed their identification. I didn't see where it said CIA, but it was definitely U.S. Government. They asked to see some identification to ascertain that I was who said I was. I had to go get some type of ID, because no one carried a wallet in Dutch Harbor. They asked a lot of questions about who I knew and what was my connection to the information. I told them about the article in the *Oceanus* and that I was familiar with the Aleutians and particularly Adak. They wanted to know what I knew about the *Glomar* and how I knew about it. I did not reveal that I knew anything about the raising of the submarine. I told them I knew about a ship out here somewhere mining for manganese nodules. I figger'd that was why they needed more pipe.

They thanked me, but refused the coffee and lunch I offered them.

I drove them back to the airport and their Learjet. They called the next day and said they wouldn't be needing the boat to deliver the pipe, as they had made other arrangements.

None of this information was available at that time. I researched the details on the dates and timing and the fact that they raised the sub and recovered the missiles and the bodies of the sailors. They gave them a military burial at sea and notified the Russians.

Others are now scraping the bottom miles below the surface and collecting these nodules that are worth millions. I knew about them 50 years ago.

What prompted this story on secrecy was watching a November 17, 2019, *60 Minutes* segment on "racing to be the first to mine trillions of dollars worth of metals used in cell phones, supercomputers and more."

There is a book called *The Codebreakers* which also speaks about secrecy. It talks about how the U.S. Navy got information on what Russians were doing on a regular basis. I read about a guy with a master's degree in electronics, specializing in listening devices, was the executive officer on the submarine that laid a listening device over the communication cable that ran from Petropavlovsk on the Kamchatka Peninsula to Vladivostok on the southeast corner of Russia, where it connects to North Korea and China. The U.S. recorded all military communications between these two submarine bases for years before the Russians discovered the device.

The information that I have written about in this story is now in the public domain.

Boat Secrets

Secrets and more, Russian top secrets galore
The Navy, the Marines, CIA, FBI and more
The secrets and mystery have to be solved
They even got Howard Hughes involved
The Russians lost a sub somewhere out there
But the U.S. Navy knows exactly where

12
Underwater Courage

King crab processing facilities in Kodiak, Alaska, after the big 1964 Good Friday earthquake and tsunami were non-existent. The wave destroyed the town and every processing plant in the area. The few processing plants that managed to get up and running were quickly overloaded. Though fishermen were eager to get out fishing, there was nowhere to deliver the crab. Cannery repair crews were shifted from their normal laid-back boring production mode into warp-speed mode to conduct whatever repairs were necessary to get the remaining plants operational.

The Alaska Packers plant had been washed off its pilings and out to sea. But they were the first to improvise a quick solution to the processing vacancies on the waterfront by removing the pilings and filling the space with rock and gravel. They leveled it and made a landing space for a World War II liberty ship, the *Kodiak Star*, to be brought in and, at high tide, moved onto the leveled gravel grid. When the liberty ship arrived, towed in by the vessel *Salvage Chief*, she was aligned with the grid and secured with cables attached to the shore and back to the *Salvage Chief*. At precisely the highest point of the tide, the 450-foot ship slid in place like it was on greased rollers. Once the ship was in the exact location and secured, they filled her tanks with water to anchor her in place. The *Salvage Chief* unhooked the cables and departed Kodiak.

The entire operation required less than four hours from the time of the *Salvage Chief*'s arrival to its departure. The *Kodiak Star* had been down south in a shipyard having a crab processing plant in-

stalled, so when it arrived she was ready to start processing crab. Of course, there were delays because of the local water, electricity, and drainage systems had to be connected. And a dock needed to be built to accommodate the offloading of the arriving crab boats.

Later, a landing craft was converted to a processor, along with a barge, a scow, and another barge, plus two old ferryboats, the *Skookum Chief* and the *Roxanne*. For companies to get back into the lucrative game of processing, it was quicker, more convenient, and much cheaper to buy old boats and scows than to build a new plant onshore. Available space for a new shore plant just wasn't there. In the coming months thousands of tons of rock were dumped into the water extending the shore seaward at road level. Shoreside space was minimal.

To eliminate the inconvenience of a floating processor rising and falling with the tide, some had grids built, and the floating processing plants were floated in on the highest tide and secured to the grids.

The grids are constructed by driving pilings into the bottom spaced about 8 feet on centers. For the *Roxanne*, the grid had to be 40 feet wide and 120 feet long. The *Roxanne* required 75 pilings. The pilings were cut off at precisely the height required to accommodate 1-foot square timbers called caps that were laid on top of the pilings and secured with long drift bolts to keep them from floating off the pilings. With the grid in place, the ferryboat-turned-processor had to be floated at the highest tide to get it high enough for her twin keels to clear the grid. The landing of the vessel on the grid was critical, and exact measurements were required, leaving no margin for error. If the contractors had measured correctly, the one-foot square caps would be precisely the height required to allow the *Roxanne* to slide right into place on the next high tide.

Divers were sent down near the keels to determine if they would clear the caps. That's where Aleutian Divers came into the picture—Marion Parker and I.

On the first above-average high tide, we stood by waiting for the peak level of tide. The *Roxanne* had been pulled alongside the grid and all the lines attached so she could be pulled sideways into place at the diver's signal of all clear.

The ferryboat's twin keels made it crucial that we verified that both keels cleared. If we got one keel on the grid and the tide started to recede before the other keel was on the caps, the hull would be punctured and the owners would be looking for another ferry.

It is one of those times when you felt the pressure of an intended successful job or unintended consequences that lead to complete failure. Marion and I didn't do failures, so we didn't take unnecessary chances. No saying, "I think it will go."

We were in position under the water. The tide peaked. But the contractors had made a mistake in their calculations. Even at high tide, the keels were about three inches from clearing the caps. It was a no-go on this tide. It became quite obvious that the *Roxanne* would require some weight removal, as she was drawing too much water.

The crab season was about to begin, and this processing company was running out of time. There were only two more big tides before the season opened!

Water tanks and fuel tanks were emptied, and everything that wasn't attached was removed from the vessel. It still wasn't enough. Marion had located some Navy surplus water bags at the Kodiak Naval Air Station. These rubber bags were about 24 feet long and 4 feet wide with separate chambers. There was a three-quarter-inch pipe running the full length of the bag that supplied water to each chamber. This pipe was about 4 inches above the outside surface of the rubber bag. Although designed to transport water, it could also be used as an airbag to raise the vessel. Then we had to determine how we were going to get it under the hull so it would stay in place while being inflated with air.

We acquired four bags thinking this would have the desired lift required for the keels to clear the caps at the next highest tide. We always had this notion that we could do anything and solve all significant problems that could possibly occur underwater. We were both well-suited to working together—as eternal optimists. This job was not our first underwater project that required radical, unorthodox equipment application.

The two bottom keels ran the full length of the *Roxanne*. They extended 4 feet below the hull, about 20 feet apart. At 8-foot intervals, the keels were supported by 3-inch struts attached to the bottom of each keel. Our plan: insert the rubber bags alongside the keels inside the struts. Sounded simple enough. However, getting a 24-foot-long rubber bag underwater proved to be somewhat more complicated than just talking about it. Our first attempt was like trying to swim with an inflated basketball to the bottom of a swimming pool. It didn't work, but it was comical!

Plan B required removing all the air from the bags. We attached a vacuum hose to the pipe that ran the length of the bag and started sucking the air from every chamber. Once the air was removed, we closed the valves, sufficiently collapsing the bag enough to eliminate the floating problem, and allowing us to sink one end and start it under the hull. Working together under the hull, pulling on the 24-foot rubber bag still wasn't working.

Plan C, however, was brilliant! We found a boat with a hydraulic winch, and the captain was willing to assist us by tying his boat on the bow end of the ferry and running a line down under the hull and attaching it to the rubber bag. The pipe that ran the length of the bag would hang up on the struts if we started pulling with the hydraulic winch. One of us would have to dive down and guide the pipe, attached to the bag, through each strut as it was being pulled by the winch. We attached a half-inch tag line along the struts to be used as a signal device. We had not yet advanced to the more modern technology of underwater telephone communications.

We finally had the bag lined up under the boat and the hauling line attached to the bag's end. I was elected to go down and guide the bag through the struts. I signaled with two jerks on the tag line to start the winch. We already had our signals set, two jerks for go ahead and one jerk for stop. We had agreed on keeping the winch slow and steady. Marion tied the other end of the tag line to his wrist so he wouldn't drop it, and also so he could feel my signal jerks on the tag line.

Everything was in place. We started hauling on the bag. I had to fold the bag by rolling the edge over to get it through the struts. As each strut came into play, I folded the edge over and then swam back to check on the last strut I had fed it through. Then I returned forward as the bag moved, feeding it through the next strut. On about the fourth strut, I was forcing the bag through, and the fold rolled over my arm and secured it like a vise, and I couldn't get my arm out! If the bag continued on, it would have pulled my left arm out of my shoulder or rolled me up like a hotdog in a bun. I managed to grab the tag line and jerked it with all the power of a maximum adrenaline rush—*just before my head was about to enter the strut.*

The bag stopped moving.

I knew they would be waiting for the two jerks that would start the bag moving again. It would be just a matter of time—soon I was hoping—before Marion determined that something was wrong and showed up with a big grin. I couldn't move my arm at all and couldn't roll my body around to see anything besides the bottom of the ferry and my feet. There was enough air in my tank for about 30 minutes, however my watch was captured in the folds of the big rubber bag on my left wrist. Feeling just a little nervous, I couldn't budge my arm, it was tight right up to my shoulder with my head against the strut. I wasn't one to panic, as I have been in tight situations before. But not this tight! So I worked to control my breathing I always do when diving. That is, take about one breath of air every thirty seconds.

What in the hell is taking them so long to figure out that we have a serious problem down here? It seemed like an hour had passed; but of course it couldn't be as I was still breathing from my tank.

I finally felt something tug on my flipper. It must be Marion because I had yet to see a giant octopus or a curious sea lion in the area. He worked his way around in front of my faceplate, and I saw his eyes widen so far I thought his eyeballs were going to fall out in his mask. I motioned to him to get me an air tank. He was gone in a split second and was back in a matter of minutes with a fresh tank. He slipped the spare tank under my right arm, and I held onto it for dear life. My backpack was a primitive aluminum tank carrier with a quick release. Just pull on the lever, and the tank would fall out. Of course, the hose feeding me air from the tank would have to go with it. Marion and I had spent many hours underwater together, and our minds worked as one, so as he jerked the tank release and slid the tank out. I took a deep breath. (I could hold my breath for 2 minutes, and he was aware of that.) He slid the tank out, removed the regulator, and let it drop to the bottom. He then grabbed the other tank from me and slipped it into the harness, attached the regulator, and fed me the mouthpiece. I inserted it and exhaled to clear the regulator, then inhaled the welcome air. I felt better already.

Marion surveyed the situation and gave me the hand signals that he would have to move the boat to the other end of the ferry and reverse the lines and connections. I gave him a thumbs up and relaxed. My only concern at that time was the fact that my left hand was starting to tingle, and that meant the circulation was slowing down.

It was taking a long time to make the changes, I thought.

Marion returned and checked my pressure gauge and gave me the sign that I had about thirty minutes before we would have to change tanks again. I could hear the boat with the winch making a move to the stern of the ferryboat. Marion was moving at warp speed. Soon he came back with another tank, and we repeated the procedure. He dropped that empty tank to the bottom and fed me the fresh one. His hand signals let me know that they were close to hooking up. Visibility was so limited I couldn't see what was going on. Marion made a connection after adjusting the collar around the bag. Then he came up to me and signaled that they were ready to pull the bag backward to release my arm. I gave him a thumb's up.

I felt the bag start to move. But then it stopped. Now what?

The hauling line broke. I guess the bag was wedged in even tighter than when we were pulling the other way. The other line must have been replaced with a stronger one, because it wasn't long before the bag started to move again—then stopped. Holy crap! What now?

Marion was back. He looked at me and wanted to know if it was okay to go ahead.

I gave him a vulgar thumbs-up. He immediately understood.

A couple of minutes later the bag moved slowly and my arm with it. At that point, I couldn't feel my arm or my hand. After about two feet back, I pulled my arm out and surfaced to breathe Kodiak's fine unpolluted air. Marion helped me out of the water, the rest of the crew cheering and clapping their hands. Tearing off my glove, I started rubbing my hand, trying to get some circulation moving, hoping that ugly blue color would go away. It wasn't long before my arm started burning and tingling with blood flow.

Marion said when I jerked that line to stop when my arm got caught, I almost pulled him overboard. He said he knew something was not right when after two minutes no further signal was received. He had grabbed his tank and ordered the crew not to move anything until he returned.

Everyone was happy to see that the situation was in good hands. We were very good at what we did, including getting in and out of trouble.

It was time to get back down there and finish the job we'd started. Marion said he would go down to feed it through the struts. But I insisted he stay topside and supervise the boat crew. Now that I had accumulated all this experience working the bag through the struts, I believed I knew best what not to do. We agreed to continue operations as before, and moved the boat with the winch back to the other end of the ferry. Both of us went down to set up the harness and collar.

That day ended with our success in getting two bags in on the port side. Once each bag was in the right position with the pipe running on the outside of the bag, they were easy to feed through the struts. Everything was set up for the next day.

We had to go back to the shop and fill the tanks and get the boat lined up ready to finish the job. We had only two more days before the maximum tide arrived.

By the time I got home, I was exhausted and too tired to eat. I immersed myself in a tub of hot water, trying to get warmth back into my hypothermic body. Several hours under 48-degree water saps your strength and burns up the calories. I don't recommend this procedure for any dieting program.

At the break of day, we were back at it, working against time and tide. It was a helluva time getting the other two bags lined up to feed into the struts. We had to pull on both ends of the bag at the same time to keep them from folding. Finally, all four bags where secured in place, and the *Roxanne* lay tight alongside the grid.

Back in the water again, I opened the valves and watched with excitement as air inflated the chambers. Loved it when a plan went together. Two hours later all the chambers were filled, and I closed the valves.

Back topside, we checked the water line on the ferry. It looked like we'd raised it about four inches. We had our doubts, but there wasn't much else we could do. We would have to wait until the next night, just before midnight, for the highest tide.

The day of reckoning arrived. We were ready in full diving regalia, awaiting the moment of truth. We had been in the water, checking things out, and we anxiously waited for the scream, "Haul her in now!"

Both of us swam under the vessel with our lights, checking the distance between the keels and the top of the grid. We would have preferred to have daylight. However, Mother Nature had decided the best tide for this perplexing maneuver was midnight—like it or not.

The port keel lay a foot from the grid just waiting for our signal. We had about a half-hour before peak tide. It looked questionable. Marion swam over to me and put his hands out as a question has formed in his brain. I motioned to surface. We held a short conversation concerning the possibilities of failure. Always the optimist and positive thinker, I said, "Bite your tongue, partner. We never fail!" He agreed and back under the boat we went.

The bottom of the keel was now even with the top of the caps. I swam the length of the keel to see if Marion's end was clear. He shined his light at the bottom of the keel.

Clear by half an inch!

We verified the other end, shining our lights on the bottom of the keel, then surface and scream, "Haul her in!"

As the ferry started to move, we dove down once more to see if the starboard keel would clear as well. It stopped. We surfaced and ask again what time was high water? We had about ten more minutes. We told them to continue holding a strain on the lines, because the starboard keel has not completely cleared. If it didn't clear, we had only a few minutes to remove the ferry off the grid, so the port keel didn't hang up on the caps.

We both swam the length of the starboard keel with our lights sweeping back and forth underneath her hull. The starboard keel cleared by half an inch. We surfaced and both scream, "Tighten her up! She's clear of the caps!"

It was as close as we ever wanted to cut it. In less than ten minutes the tide receded enough to set the *Roxanne* solidly on the grid.

The crew cheered!

Marion and I were grinning from ear to ear.

As I have said before, "I just love it when a plan goes together."

Of course, then we still had to remove the bags from beneath the keel. It had to be done at high water, so we could float them out after removing enough air to slide them through the struts but leave enough air in the chambers to float them. It wasn't a critical rush, so we decided to rest up for a couple of days and do our work at high tide in daylight hours.

Just another day and night in the life of a commercial diver.

Underwater Courage

A ferry boat still afloat, purchased for the highest bid
It's gonna be a processor after it's set on the grid
The grid is built by engineers and all are very skilled
Two divers have to get it up there and not get killed
The question is will it fit as no space to clear
I doubt it, let's go have a beer

13
Mayday!

The U.S. Coast Guard HH-3F Pelican helicopter stationed out of Kodiak was sent on a nighttime search and rescue mission to assist a vessel that had managed to blast off one—and only one—"Mayday!" on their marine radio. Under normal circumstances a vessel in trouble will call three times "Mayday! Mayday! Mayday!" and instantly follow up with the vessel name, location, and the problem.

This radio transmission caused great concern for all who heard that one "Mayday," because the call could have come from one mile or a thousand miles away in any direction. Fortunately, Dan Hanson, the captain on the fishing vessel *Half Moon Bay*, had heard the Mayday distress call as well, having just talked to Jerry ("Corky") Tilley Jr., the captain of the fishing distressed vessel *El Rancho* a while before, and Captain Hanson recognized Captain Corky's voice. A "Mayday relay call" was heard by the *Half Moon Bay*, the Japanese fishing vessel *Daishin Maru 28*, and the Coast Guard cutter *Rush*, a high-endurance cutter out of Honolulu, which performed regular patrols in the Gulf of Alaska. That is how the Coast Guard station in Kodiak received the call. The location was relayed to the Coast Guard via Captain Hanson, who knew the distressed *El Rancho*'s approximate position.

The *El Rancho* had just finished the baridi crab season on day 10 west of Kodiak Island. After depositing 30,000 pounds of these crustaceans into the live tank, the four-man crew had loaded the last of their crab pots aboard and secured them to the railings and the deck with chains and chain binders. A chain binder is a device used to pull the chain as tight as possible; the lever on the chain binder is then locked down to the binder. If the lever slipped out of your hand and part of your body was in the way of that lever, it could break your arm or knock you overboard.

The weather was typical for February in western Alaska. It had been storming, with 40–50 knot winds and the seas running 10 to 12 feet. The *El Rancho* had been anchored up behind Sutwik Island, west of Kodiak Island, waiting for the weather to calm down so they could get to Kodiak and offload the crab pots. The 30,000 pounds of crab in the vessel's hold was going to give the crew some much-needed funds, and they were anxious to sell.

About 7:30 a.m., the faint light of the approaching day crept over the eastern horizon, and they could see the storm had reduced its intensity and the seas appeared to be tolerable. Captain Corky decided it was time to go, so they weighed anchor, secured it in the hawse pipe, and left the calmer area behind the island. Steering into the left-over storm's turbulent seas, he set a course for Cape Alitak on the southwestern end of Kodiak Island, about 120 miles away.

The crew of four were experienced fishermen. Mike Mark from Eagle, Idaho, was the biggest sailor aboard. Brian Fletcher, Gerry Hovis, Brian Kelly, and the captain were from Westport, Washington. Captain Corky was 30 years old and had been fishing since he could stand up on a rolling deck, before he had even reached his teens.

An 82-foot steel vessel, the *El Rancho* had excellent stability. Each crewman stood a three-hour wheel watch maintaining the given compass course. As the boat plowed through the swells, everyone had accepted the fact that it was not going to be a smooth ride to Cape Alitak.

Not too far along on their journey, the sun set at 5:30 p.m., a typical February in the North Pacific. *So far so good.*

The seas were running 6 to 10 feet with 30-knot winds. The cook always had a something prepared regardless of the condition of the sea. He managed to put a meal together in the rocking, rolling galley, then called the crew to supper. They finished eating and crawled into their bunks to get some sleep.

Captain Corky returned to the wheelhouse and took over the watch. On the marine radio, he had a conversation with Dan Hanson, on the *Half Moon Bay*, and mentioned his location and the nasty weather they were encountering about 40 miles from Cape Alitak.

An hour or so after signing off from talking to Hanson, Corky noticed the vessel was a little sluggish to return to even keel on the rolls. After you've been on a boat for any length of time, you come to feel the action of the vessel at sea, the particular sounds of the engine, the vibrations through the hull. You quickly learn how the boat reacts when plowing into a large swell or rolling off one. You can tell right away if something's not right.

Corky noticed they were heaving too far to starboard, so he secured the helm and left the wheelhouse to go down and tell the engineer to transfer fuel from the starboard fuel tank to the port fuel tank, adjusting the ballast. The engineer said he was already doing that. Corky told him to go double check. Then he woke the crew up and told them to don survival suits and get up to the wheelhouse. Mike Mark's assignment was to get up on top of the wheelhouse and stand by to release the life raft.

Corky's biggest worry was maybe the boat *wasn't* sinking. He had heard stories of crews abandoning ship and the boat *not* sinking but rather floating off and ending up grounded on a beach somewhere. It had happened before: a boat on the beach, life raft missing, the crew never found. His thinking was justified. He was waiting until the last minute to call "abandon ship."

Noticing the stern way too low in the water, and hearing loud crashes below deck, Corky glanced over at the inclinometer, which read 25-degree list to portside. At that moment everyone in wheelhouse realized, almost too late, that the *El Rancho* was sinking.

Corky ordered the crew into their survival suits!

The life raft was readied. One last time into the wheelhouse, Corky, survival suit in hand, grabbed up the radio mic and called out "Mayday . . ." but he didn't even have time to radio the other two "Maydays"—the boat started to roll over!

Corky barely made it out the wheelhouse door before the *El Rancho* rolled over completely onto its side. Corky saw Brian Fletcher stumbling down the side of the boat yelling, "I can't do it!" Understandably he feared jumping into that violent, dark, freezing water. Again he hollered at his captain, "I can't jump in!"

Corky managed to get into his survival suit, not a simple task even in light seas. The sinking boat still provided enough light so he could see to grab the painter line. This "painter" line is attached to the life raft's canister on one end, and the other end is attached to the boat. When a vessel goes down, the painter line is pulled out of its container on the canister. When the line reaches the end, it is supposed to release the attachment that opens the canister—and out pops the life raft. This process started just as the boat rolled over completely and slipped beneath the waves!

They were left in total darkness.

Fletcher's no-jump decision had been made for him, and he was splashing in the water—but a ways from where the rest of the crew were huddling together. Corky had been pulling on the painter line until he had it wrapped around his arms and his head. Now he struggled to breathe as waves crashed down on him. He was thinking he was lost when Mark grabbed hold of him and helped pull the painter line out the rest of the way—*but the canister didn't open*!

In desperation, Corky rolled over on his back, got both feet against the canister, jerked as hard as he could, and canister opened.

The raft instantly expanded with air and the light on top shone bright, illuminating an area of crashing 10-foot seas, 30-knot winds, and 30-degree air temperature. The 40-degree water made any effort to accomplish anything prodigiously difficult.

Getting into a life raft's opening is not easy in the big seas and howling winds that buffeted the raft away. Nonetheless, they all managed to get into the raft. Except Brian Fletcher.

They all saw him struggling out on the perimeter of the raft's light at the height of one wave, and then disappearing behind another. He was riding up and down on the swells, and he kept yelling, "I can't make it!"

"Swim to us!" everyone yelled back to him. "You *can* make it!"

Hovis jumped back in the water, swam out to Fletcher and dragged him back to the raft. Swimming in a survival suit is like swimming with your bunk mattress tied to your back!

Finally, everyone was aboard. Corky dug out the flares.

The mayday call having been received and relayed, and the approximate location of the *El Rancho* determined, the Coast Guard station in Kodiak had their helicopter warming up and a C-130 Hercules also cranking its engines. The HH-3F Pelican lifted off and headed for the south end of Kodiak Island. On a straight line it was 130 miles to the *El Rancho*'s last location. A Pelican can fly at 140 knots and cruise at 120, so they were a little over an hour away depending on head-winds. The C-130 took off shortly after that. It arrived on the scene before the helicopter, cruising at around 290 knots. With a reasonably accurate location, they were on the scene in less than half an hour.

The men in the raft managed to set off a rocket parachute flare. Soon afterwards, they made out the blinking lights of the C-130 circling overhead. The C-130 guided the helicopter to the exact coordinates.

An hour later, at 9:18 p.m., the crew of the *El Rancho* saw the chopper holding position overhead. The helicopter crew lowered the rescue retrieving basket to the raft as it rose up and down with the swell. The wind swung the rescue basket back and forth over the raft.

Captain Corky eventually got all the crew safely off the raft and up to the chopper.

The chopper lowered the basket one last time for Corky, 90 minutes since the *El Rancho* had gone down.

Corky tried to get the basket under him to roll into it, but a heavy swell and a wind gust didn't allow him to make it into the basket. Before he could signal the helicopter that he wasn't ready, up it went with him just barely hanging on. He lost his grip and fell back into the raging sea.

He landed on his back with a shock, the wind knocked out of him. With a monumental amount of determination and physical endurance, Corky managed to swim back to the drifting raft, grab hold of it with one arm over the entrance lip, and hang on trying to catch his breath.

The chopper crew again lowered the basket, despite wind and swell. Exhausted, dazed, and out of breath, one last time Corky tried to wave the chopper away because the basket was swinging too close to him and he feared getting hit in the head before he could get into it.

With no recollection of how he had managed it, Corky realized he was a hundred feet in the air getting closer to the helicopter's door. Once inside, his crew greeted their captain with joy, happy

Coast Guard rescues 5 from sinking crabber

By RICHARD HARTMAN
Staff Writer

All five crewmen off the 82-foot fishing vessel El Rancho were safe this morning after their boat sank last night 35 miles west of Cape Alitak, reports said.

Five crab fishermen arrive safely at the Coast Guard base last night after their vessel, El Rancho, sank in 6-10-foot seas 35 miles west of Cape Alitak. The Air Station at Kodiak launched an H-3 copter and C-130 airplane to the scene of the sinking at about 8:30 last night and hoisted the El Rancho crewmen from their life raft where they had spent about an hour's time. Photo by PA2 Rick Woods, U.S. Coast Guard.

they were not all visiting with Davey Jones as so many had before them!

After a bone-chilling ride in wet clothes to the Kodiak Coast Guard base, barefooted with only shirts and Levi's, they were all assisted off the helicopter and delivered to the base infirmary to get checked out. Everything they owned had gone down with the *El Rancho*.

Had Dan Hanson not talked to the *El Rancho* and then heard that "Mayday," there would be no telling what the next problem would have been for that life raft of five cold, wet sailors. Later, Dan Hanson told Corky that after hearing just one "Mayday" and nothing more, he'd feared the worst. He thought they had all gone down.

The crew and captain were released from the Coast Guard infirmary and taken to the Shelikof Inn to spend the rest of the night. Then back to Westport to find another boat, once more to go fishing in the Gulf of Alaska. This is the way of the commercial fisherman.

Thanking the U.S. Coast Guard for their immediate response was the order of the day.

Mayday!

The trip is nasty, long, and overdue
Captain's at the wheel, asleep are the crew
The boat is rolling and slow on the return
Too low in the water, down in the stern
Blowing forty and a huge swell
We are not gonna make it
I can tell

14
Kalakala Challenge

I just can't refuse a chance to do something no one else has done before.

Northern Processors was a seafood processing company with three floating facilities located in and around Kodiak Island. I was the general manager. Just to complicate things, the vice president of Vita Foods out of Seattle arrived in Kodiak and offered me a job. He wanted me to build a shrimp and crab processing operation on a World War II liberty ship that Vita Foods had bought out of the fleet of WWII vessels located in Olympia, Washington. The *Thomas Bullfinch* was 450 feet long and had been towed to an empty dock and warehouse on the waterfront in Tacoma, which was large enough for trucks delivering material—without fear of falling through the old decking. The *Thomas Bullfinch*'s color was Navy gray ugly. However, she was in like-new condition and fit right in with the surrounding area of lost maritime businesses, oddly nowhere near a shipyard where you would think they would want to do the conversion. They hired a crew of experts to assist—carpenters, welders, painters, electricians, sheet metal operators, pipefitters, bull-shitters, *and me*.

I was not too sure I wanted to leave Kodiak. It had been my home town for ten years, and I just got married two months before. The pay would be half of what I was presently making. But I was never one to turn down a project that would require something new. My eternal optimism won out. I accepted the job.

We packed most everything getting ready to leave when I received a call from Phil Harris, the superintendent of Bob Resoff's shrimp cannery on the old Seattle ferry *Kalakala*. It was pulled ashore in Gibson Cove about a half a mile south of Kodiak city dock.

Phil Harris was the nicest guy you would ever meet. He asked me if I would come down to his plant and see what the problem with his pipeline was. This pipeline pumped the shrimp processing waste into the current outside Gibson Cove.

A few months back, the engineer for the operation was in town and wanted a meeting with divers. There were three divers at the meeting when he introduced the pipeline project. He wanted bids on laying 1,500 feet of 40-foot lengths of 8-inch pipe from the *Kalakala* to outside Gibson Cove. I asked him what he was going to use for anchors. He looked at me like I was not of his caliber and below his station in life. He said, "It is a steel pipe. Steel doesn't float." I have no idea what kind of engineer this guy would classify himself, but he wasn't of my caliber. I thought to myself that I had better leave now before I open my usual sarcastic big mouth. I left.

I told Phil Harris to call Willie, the diver who got the contract and laid the pipe, to check it out. Phil said he left town with the $40,000 he received for the job. I told Phil I was packed and ready to leave town. My diving partner was in Bristol Bay, working on another project. Phil was just about in tears because he had two shrimp boats wanting to unload. I told him I would get my gear and be back soon. He had closed the plant because the pipeline was spewing waste in the inner cove. I returned and walked out to the edge and jumped in. I went down to the bottom and followed the pipe out about two lengths, and that was the end of the pipe. I could see where the pipe had been moving back and forth on the bottom. There were deep grooves where it had been going from side to side and up and down like a huge sea monster breaking out of confinement. Picture your garden hose when you turn it on. If you don't have hold of it, away it goes. When the waste receiving

tank is pumped down to empty, air is pumped into the pipeline. Steel pipe floats when air is pumped into it.

The pipe had broken the connections and separated. The 40-foot lengths of pipe disengaged and each length of pipe just took off in all directions.

The pipe was scattered all over the bottom. I went back and climbed out on the dock and told Phil the bad news. He couldn't believe it.

They were out of business because the pipe was spewing shrimp waste all across the surface of Gibson Cove. I told Phil there were no anchors on the pipe. He said, "Can you fix it?" "Phil, I just told you. I am packed and leaving for a new job in Tacoma, and we are leaving next week." I felt terrible for Phil, and there was no other alternative for him or his boats. I said, "Okay, Phil, I will put your pipeline back together." He asked me how long it would take to do that. It had taken Willie two months to lay it out. I told him I could do it in a week. He got a big grin on his face and said, "In case you don't know it, Jerry, you are not a young man." I was 39 and in excellent physical condition. He was still laughing while walking away. We got serious at the meeting with my diving gear still on. I told him what I wanted him to do.

I told him to get a crew making saddles using web and rocks. I need 75–80 pounds or more on each side so I can drop them on the pipe with rocks on both sides. I told him to start with a hundred saddles. I need a raft and a tender at all times. I need someone filling air tanks. I went home and told my new wife Joann what I was going to do. I had a raft large enough to hold a couple of guys and equipment. They still had the raft that Willie used. I rigged a pipe seal for the ends of the pipe so I could insert air and float the sections of pipe where I would need to make the connections. The pipe had to be perfectly lined up to the other end to put the connectors on. The flanges were near impossible to connect without help. I managed to complete the task using two chain hoists. I worked underwater for 8 hours every day for 5 days. When I would get home, Joann had to help me get out of my wet suit because my hands were numb from the cold water and I couldn't feel the zippers. The skin was missing from the back of my knees, the crook of my elbows, and my armpits. Blood would run out of my suit. The constant pulling, swimming, getting all the pipe in place, jacking the handle on the chain hoist, and wrenching the flange bolts rubbed me raw. I used eight tanks of air every day. I completed the job in 5 days. I charged them $50 an hour. I got a check for $2,000. No one would believe I did that job in 5 days by myself. Phil was the happiest guy in town and laid so much praise on me, I could hardly walk.

Kalakala Challenge

A chance to prove who you are
People know me from afar
Because this is what I do
I love doing new

15
100-Foot Drop

February is not the best time to fly from the Pacific Northwest to the frozen Siberian tundra and beyond. But when work calls, we must earn our pay.

I wasn't too excited about leaving Seattle, as I had just returned from cold and windy Dutch Harbor, where we had the Russian vessel *Starzhinsky* in for fueling. I hadn't warmed up from that trip, and now I was departing again back to the cold.

Bogdon Nalivaiko, our co-manager at Marine Resources Company International, joined me for the trip to act as my interpreter. We boarded an Alaska Airlines flight from Seattle to Anchorage, then on to Khabarovsk in the Russian far east. We arrived at midnight, the temperatures hovering around zero. We spent the rest of the night in the airport, then waited for a flight to Petropavlovsk. In the morning, two guys from Severo-Kurilsk, interpreter Bogdon, and I boarded the Russian version of a passenger plane, which I referred to as Aeroshot instead of Aeroflot. There were delays after delays, but we started our taxi run from the gate to the main runway—*then we stopped*. The plane held there on the taxiway and we waited. I had a window seat and watched as a fuel truck pumped gas from nearby aircraft parked off the taxiway, then drove over to our plane, unfurled its hose, attached it to the fuel inlet on the wing, and pumped the fuel into our plane. I wondered if this was standard operating procedure in Russia.

Fortunately, we had enough fuel to get us to Petropavlovsk-Kamchatskiy during daylight. The temperature was −7. We had many more delays. The chopper we were supposed to ride on to our final destination left without us. I was ready for a nap. No other choice but to get to the hotel and wait for the next day. Jet lag had a detrimental effect on my sleep program, so I was awake most of the night. We managed to get to the heliport at noon, then waited until 3:15 p.m. to board, because they were not sure about the weather at our destination.

Inside the helicopter, full fuel tanks doubled as passenger seats.

The chopper was a typical Russian 4-blade rotor that felt like one blade was missing—the vibration was rather severe. There were two gas tanks, one on each side of the outside of the aircraft; and there were two more gas tanks on the inside of the cabin. I noticed passengers smoking right next to both inside tanks!

The chopper started to lift off, then dropped back to the ground. Three times it went up, then back down. Made one wonder about the flight possibilities. Finally, we were airborne and heading south towards the southern tip of the Kamchatka Peninsula.

Looking out the window at the snow-covered tundra below, I thought, If this unit fell out of the air, we were going to be very cold.

About an hour and a half out, we hit heavy snow. The pilot kept going past the town of Ozernovskiy for about 15 minutes, but soon turned around and landed on a hill south of town. We waited half an hour, daylight beginning to fade. We then lifted off to land again down the hill closer to the town. We waited there until 7:00 p.m.

Finally, someone came to us, accompanied by the director of the *kolkhoz*, a collective fishing enterprise. We got off the chopper, treading through a foot or more of snow, and climbed into the patrol 4x4. From the kolkhoz office, Bogdon and I were driven to the director's apartment for supper, after which we were taken to a dorm in another building. I slept the night in my clothes.

Next day was reasonably clear, but inclement farther south. The people that made decisions there arranged for us to board a factory

trawler that would take us to Severo-Kurilsk. We went to a pier on the river, then boarded a tug that took us out to a ship waiting for us offshore.

The tug sliced its way through the ice accumulation on the river's freshwater layer and hit bottom three times before we were out through the little bit of surf to the factory trawler. It seemed that we were going a little too fast for a soft landing. The tug rammed the side of the ship, sheared off, then rammed it again, and bounced off twice more. At last, the tug attached a line so we could climb the ladder to the deck of the trawler. I accepted this maneuver as normal.

Away we went to Severo-Kurilsk. On the way, we stopped and offloaded a trawler's 25 tons of fish to be processed on board as we traveled. I was in the wheelhouse with the captain when he pointed and said, "There is the town of Severo-Kurilsk." I said, "Where?" I saw the masts of the few vessels in the harbor, but that was all I saw. He pointed and said, "There. Here, take these binoculars and look for the chimneys sticking out of the snow."

On arrival offshore, we boarded another smaller boat for the remainder of the trip to the pier in the harbor. We were picked up in a half-track and taken to a tiny hotel. We climbed down the snow steps to the front door and were shown to our rooms. It was not warm. We went to bed for some much-needed rest. No supper, so out comes my beef jerky and mixed nuts. We had a meeting scheduled for 9:00 in the morning. At 3:30 in the morning the lights started blinking, got dim, then went out.

We were up and ready for our appointed time and meeting, so Bogdon and I went to the front door and opened it to a solid wall of snow. We took the shovel that was right inside the door and started shoveling the snow into the entrance until we could climb out and make a hole so we could shovel the snow out of the inside of the hotel lobby back out the door and up on top. We managed to build some steps so we could climb out in-

stead of crawling out like a bear after its hibernation was over. Our pick-up crew was delayed, maybe on purpose so they wouldn't have to shovel their way into the hotel to get us. We were in Russia so we didn't get too excited about delays in schedule times.

We were driven to the boat harbor area, where we entered the building where they wanted us to make the changes. Their goal was to redesign the plant to be able to process other seafoods besides what the plant was designed for. While I was crawling around the equipment measuring and drawing the layout, I had to shoo the rats away. Some came a foot away from my nose. The rats were not afraid of me. We managed to complete our surveys and suggested details for a change in their plant. We had some meetings that day and into the evening, then back to the hotel to get ready to leave tomorrow.

No. We were not leaving because there was no helicopter. The weather had deteriorated and snow was arriving sideways at 30-plus knots. In the hotel, there was very little light because the electrical system has not been repaired. We had no idea why, but we did know when there was no electricity, there was no heat. The hotel did not have a kitchen, so no food was served. Bogdon and I went out and cruised around the small town looking for somewhere to eat. We found a small place in a big apartment building that looked like they might have some food. We went in and sat down at a small table. Bogdon called to someone in Russian, of course, and a lady came out from the back. They talked, and Bogdon looked at me and asked if a couple of pieces of fish would be okay?

He said, "That's all they have." We had a couple of chunks of codfish and some tea. That was supper, and lunch was some salmon roe and bread. Now we were in for another night. Maybe tomorrow we could get out of here. During the night we had an earthquake. It didn't shake me out of my cot but it certainly woke me up. I couldn't see if there was any damage because it was dark and no electricity. I had a mag flashlight but didn't even bother to get up and look around. If the roof and a ton of snow didn't land on me, I had determined there was no need for me get out of a warm bed to look around. No sound was heard from Bogdon. I think he didn't feel it. At least, it didn't wake him.

During the afternoon the wind picked up to about 50–60 miles per hour and snow was trying to hit the ground but was being blown too fast to stop and stick. Lots of snow. It was piling up around the buildings and our doorway. Part of the new roof on one of the buildings in the harbor blew off. The roof over the new swimming pool collapsed. There was not enough light in the hotel to read a book. I went out the door with the shovel and started digging a hole down to the window so I could get enough light that would allow me to read. The next day we walked about 2 miles in the snow where it had been packed down by the half-track. That was the only transportation in town. So far, we had no food. We went back to the hotel and waited for some news, good news preferably. The door opened, and the hotel manager came in with a one-unit propane burner and a big pot. He set it down, attached the fuel hose, set the pot of water on the burner, and waited for the water to boil. I was wondering what was going into the pot, thinking it may be a dead fish—even a fish head would suffice at this point. I was wrong. It was a package of noodles. Nothing else went in the pot. No bread, no salmon roe to go with it, just noodles. That was supper.

The chopper arrived the next morning and landed in an accessible area clear of visible buildings and sank into the snow to the belly of the aircraft. We were packed and ready to go. We trudged through the snow to the helicopter. We waited for a short while and the snow returned in force. Back to the hotel. Another night and still no electricity.

The helicopter crew joined us at the hotel. We experienced another minor earthquake during the night of Valentine's Day. I didn't get up for this one either. There was no need to get up before we had some daylight because there was no electricity and I didn't have night-vision goggles. When I finally decided to arise from the warmth of the blankets, it was because I thought we might be able to leave here. I was out of beef jerky and mixed nuts. Only one small packet of instant oatmeal remained.

That morning, we made it back to the chopper. It was covered with snow. The helicopter crew managed to clear off most of it and then got inside and cranked it up. There were two pilots and a third man. We didn't know why the third man was always with the pilots. I thought that maybe he was their instructor. We waited along with several others who were there hoping for a ride to Petropavlovsk. Finally, they told us to board. I was the first one in because if it was going anywhere, I was certainly going to be there with it. Bogdon followed me in. I sat right by the door, and Bogdon sat beside me. I was right behind the pilots. We both had a suitcase. Then the others climbed aboard. The door was closed. Everyone was seated, but there were not enough seats for all, so some were sitting on the fuel tanks. All, except for the third man, who was always standing behind the two pilots.

Then the pilot started the rotor going, and as it increased, he varied the blades for lift. There was no lift. He tried a couple more times but no lift. "Okay," the third man called out. "Everybody off." I got out and everyone followed. We were told to stay clear of the aircraft, so we all moved away from the rotor blades. Then they cranked it up with enough power to lift it out of the snow, which caused a blizzard effect on those of us standing away. The aircraft made it about a hundred yards towards the water, then the pilot sat it down on a hill. We were told to get aboard. We trudged and crawled through the snow and climbed in. We all looked like snowmen, only without the carrot nose and the coal eyes. I was so thankful for my down parka. The blades started and wound up enough to lift off—but no lift. The wheels are buried in the snow. "Everybody off!" came the cry from the third man. Everybody got off except me. I stayed because I was not going to be covered by blowing snow like before. Bogdon got off even after I told him to remain seated. I guess the agitated verbal display of the third man was probably telling us to get off, but I didn't move. The third man gave me a dirty look and pointed to the door. I shook my head, no. They cranked it up and got it clear of the grip the snow had on the wheels and undercarriage.

We managed to move it a little higher on the edge of a cliff where the wind had cleared the snow away. Here came the snowmen trudging and half-crawling through the snow to board. Bogdon looked like he had rolled to the doorway. I brushed some of the snow off so he wouldn't be sitting on a pile of snow. All aboard and ready for lift-off. Now, the weight of everyone may have had some effect on this thing not only getting off the snow pack but flying. The pilot wound it up and gave the blades the necessary angle of pitch for lift-off, but again no lift.

He tried a couple more times, and I was sure we were going to abandon this trip all together. We were sitting right on the edge of the wind-blown cliff, and the chopper was rocking from the wind. The third man, who was always standing behind the two pilots, reached in and pulled the pilot out of his seat and stood him up where he had been standing. Then he sat down in the pilot's empty seat. He grabbed the controls, wound that engine up to a roaring, screaming velocity, twisted the rotor control, and we bounced a couple times before we went over the cliff straight down to the rocks and water. Now was the time to ask God to forgive all my sins and send my guardian angel, like right now.

We plummeted with hardly any lift, and then about 20 feet off the surface of the rocks and the Sea of Okhotsk, the helicopter achieved lift. We started to gain some altitude. I looked over at Bogdon and thought maybe he had died, because he was as white as a sheet, his eyeballs were stationary, and his mouth was half open as if he was about to say something or scream, but no words came out. Now we were airborne thanks to the third man and his helicopter expertise. I saw that some color had returned to Bogdon and his mouth had closed. Then I mentioned that we must be low on fuel after flying here from Ozernovskiy and all the warming up and trying to get airborne. He just looked at me and said nothing.

Now we are over water and heading for the island closer to the Kamchatka Peninsula. The angle of flight was dropping us closer to the next island instead of over it. Down we went and landed right next to a large fuel tank. We were about out of gas. The weather had improved significantly and the sky was clear. The third man announced everybody off the helicopter. I was the first out the door, and the snow was the same level as the door. The aircraft had sunk to its belly in the soft, newly fallen snow. I sank to my knees. When we were all off, the pilot lit a cigarette, inhaled deeply, walked over to the outboard fuel tanks and pulled the lid off, and looked in—with the cigarette hanging from his lip. I grabbed Bogdon, and we moved away, way away.

Before too long here came a guy on a snow machine. He was the caretaker of the emergency fuel depot. Here was the best part, Bogdon knew this guy. So Bogdon asked him if we could use his snow machine while he fueled up the chopper. "No problem," he said, so we jumped on this ancient-looking thing, and away we went up the hill. We came to the remains of a World War II hangar and the wing of an American airplane sticking out of the snow. There was obviously some history here, but I could only imagine why it was here. We returned to the helicopter, and the fueling was completed without an explosion or other accident. We all boarded the aircraft, closed the door, and proceeded with the startup program. Wound it up, twisted the pitch control, and went nowhere.

The third man got out of the pilot's seat and again instructed everybody to get off. Not me or Bogdon. Now they must get it up and over to an area with no snow, while it is a little lighter. However, the fuel we just pumped into the tanks has added some serious weight. We managed to get out of the snow and over to the hill right by the cliff where the snow has been removed by Mother Nature's wind off the Sea of Okhotsk.

All the poor souls left by the fuel tanks slowly high-stepped and partially crawled through the snow to our new location. The rest of the snow-laden passengers were aboard once again. The third man was at the controls and repeated the identical procedure to get it airborne as before. Two bounces and then over the cliff as we plummeted once again towards the water and the rocks below. This time the pilot managed to level off just about a 100 feet from the surface of the sea. I could not even call this one a close encounter with the rocks. Onward to Petropavlovsk, arriving there in daylight. We

couldn't land at the airport because the landing area had not been cleared. So, we landed in an open lot close to a road. He set it down gently and it settled to its belly in the snow. I was first out and sank to my crotch. I grabbed my suitcase and swam with it in front of me until I reached the berm of the road, which is about 5 feet high. I rolled over it and crashed to the road below with my suitcase. I stood up and looked at the aircraft and watched Bogdon crawl over my trail to the road. We made it to a hotel located nearby and called our office to come and get us. We were ready for some food. I have had many hours in helicopters, as I had been delivered to different areas and offshore jobs as a commercial diver in Alaska. This trip was a bit different than the ones I was used to when traveling by helicopter. However, any new experience is always welcome.

100-Foot Drop

Kamchatka in the winter is not a winner ya know
I am the one that has been requested to go
I take my Russian translator, Mr. Bogdon Nalivaiko
The helicopter looks old and the paint is peeling
We climb aboard but have a weird feeling
Lift off into the cold and blowing snow
Start our flight to where we are to go
Vibration is rather severe
Whoa, we can't land this thing here

16 Dynamite

The King crab boat pulled in and tied up to the unloading dock. The captain climbed onto the dock and mentioned that he had hit something coming in. He said it was not a hard hit but felt it scrape the bottom. He asked me to dive down and check to see if there was any damage.

At the bottom of his boat, I could see where something had scraped and removed the paint. I surfaced and told him that he was right. Then I decided to take a cruise across the bottom area where he said he thought he felt the bump. I jumped off the dock, swam down trying to see in the murky water what he could have hit. There rose up a pinnacle of rock from the bottom with part of the top scraped off, clearly by more than one boat.

It was not in the channel but off to the side away from the traffic pattern, right in line with any boat maneuvering to get alongside the dock to unload. It was also the home of an octopus. There was a pile of empty crab and clam shells outside a small cave at the bottom of the rock. I stuck in my arm. The octopus probed a tentacle along my arm and out to my dive tank. It didn't want to come out and meet me. It was just saying hello.

Back at the dock, I climbed up the ladder, and dropped my tank, regulator, and weight belt. The boat's captain came over to me. "So, what do ya think?" he asked. I pointed out the route he could take to avoid the underwater hazard. "What would it take to remove the obstruction?"

"It's a big rock," I explained. "Looks porous, not like solid granite. Got a 3- to 4-foot diameter base, maybe 6 feet high." I said it reminded me of an ice cream cone some kid dropped upside-down. "And there's a hole in in the base, with a good-sized octopus livin' in there."

The captain thanked me and went back to work. I dove down one more time to get a better look, wondering what I could do to remove the hazard. The octopus scooted away into its hole when I arrived. "Octo" was not small, its tentacles well over three feet long. After reviewing the rock, stabbing at its surface with my knife to no effect, I concluded it would take a lot more than a diver's knife to break it up.

I paid a visit to the harbormaster to see if he had any ideas. He suggested setting a marker buoy over it. But that wouldn't last long, because it was right in line with Kodiak Airway's floatplane ramp. At the Navy Base I was directed to Captain James Spargo, base commander. I apprised him of the situation, suggesting the Corps of Engineers might be able to look into it, being a local shipping lane hazard. "Even at a medium tide," I noted, "the rock could rip a hole in a boat." They'd get back to me in a few days, I was told. In the meantime, I informed our crab boats where the rock was hiding and advised them to schedule arrival at high tide if at all possible.

The next down day of processing, Marion Parker, my dive partner at Aleutian Divers, and I once more went to check out the rock. Octo was getting friendly. He came out and wrapped his tentacles around my head and arms. That was okay, until he slithered one of those suction-cup covered tentacles across my face mask and air regulator mouthpiece. That was not funny! I tried to pull the tentacles off, and the facemask came with it. I bit down on my mouthpiece to keep it in place. My partner was having a good laugh. I retrieved my mask and put it back on. Then Octo—I estimated him at 50 to 60 pounds—slithered off into his den.

We swam around the obstruction several times and tried to get Octo out of his den so we could see how deep and how far back it went. Old Octo refused to come out, and that was that.

Back on the dock, we discussed ideas for how to get rid of the rock. I suggested dynamite, having been a powder monkey when I worked in the woods as a younger guy—a *much* younger guy—blowing stumps for building roadways in the logging camps. Dynamite was not dangerous when used in the area around or under a stump; it is stable in diatomaceous earth. And the nitro does not leak out unless it is left for long periods in damp earth. I knew more about dynamite than what was required to blow this rock.

The Corps of Engineers still hadn't returned any of my calls. Marion and I decided something had to be done, though he was not too keen on my idea of using dynamite. In water, if not used quickly, the nitro will leak out into the water and become unstable, possibly blowing up on its own.

I went to Fred Brechan at Brechan Construction and asked him for a case of 60 percent ditching powder and a couple of electric blasting caps. I think there were 60 sticks of powder in a case. He asked me, "What in the hell are you gonna do with it?" I explained in detail what I had in mind. Then he wanted to ascertain that I knew how to use this stuff. "I spent a year blowing up stumps, rock quarries, log jams, and hillsides," I told him. "Oh, and can you keep it stored in the WWII concrete bunker until I am ready?" I asked. I also asked him not to tell anyone what I planned. Back in those days you didn't need special permits and licenses to get dynamite. He agreed, requesting a day's notice before I came to pick it up.

Now I had to give this operation a lot of thought. I didn't want anyone to know until I had the rock prepared to blast. I discovered Marion didn't want to have anything to do with me and dynamite, especially underwater! I'd be on my own, so I'd do my diving in the morning at first light, at 3:30 a.m. The waters were fairly shallow, so visibility would be good.

I dove down to visit old Octo and see if I could get him to move to another location, because I wanted to use his den to plant the case of dynamite. Octo didn't like the idea of moving, so I had to bribe him with King crab legs. Every boat that delivered crab always had a few that died in route, which they tossed overboard. Waving crab legs in front of the octopus, it was only a minute before a tentacle appeared and grabbed what I offered. I hung onto the bribe until Octo slid all the way out of its hole for a visit. Soon the beast was crawling all over me. Octo seemed to love covering my head but seldom ever wrapped around my dive tank. I think it did not like the feel of metal.

I made several dives to the rock with dead crab trying to get the stubborn creature away from its den. Octo became more and more friendly. Each time I showed up, he came slithering out and wrapped me up. I think he was telling me, "Thank you, but no I ain't leaving my den!"

All I seemed to be accomplishing was making Octo heavier and stronger by feeding him all that crab, and I was running out of time!

The day was getting late, but I managed to get Octo out of the den, feeding him a crab that I hung onto until he was completely clear. With his tentacles secured to the crab, I swam away down the channel and let go. Racing back his den, I saw that Octo had quite an accumulation of empty shells piled inside. But there was also plenty of room for the dynamite.

The very next morning, I dropped off the dock and swam out to visit Octo. As I neared the den here came Octo looking for his breakfast. I had no breakfast, but that didn't stop him—and I had to laugh inside my mask—he was all over me searching for crab.

Later I called the Navy base to talk to Captain Spargo. I wanted to know what if anything the Corps of Engineers had to say about what I was planning. Captain Spargo was not on base, so I received no information.

Determined to complete my plan as soon as possible, I called Fred Brechan and told him I would pick up the case of dynamite the next day, which was a Friday. I spent the rest of the day, planning just how I was going to do the job alone. Negative thoughts were tossed out like a dead crab; only room for positive thoughts about how well things would go.

Saturday morning I drove to the dock. I had my wet suit on, and my other gear in the truck. There was no one around at 2:30 a.m., and dawn brought but a hint of sunlight. I took the case of dynamite out of the front seat, and grabbed a chunk of crab line from the back, securing it to the case of dynamite so it wouldn't slip out and crash to the surface of the water before I was ready. Didn't want it to get it wet before absolutely necessary. Dynamite at that time came in a waxed cardboard case with the contents covered in waxed paper. I slowly lowered the case to just above the water and tied it off. I took the blasting caps and a roll of wire with me, and jumped in, then swam over to the box of dynamite and released it from my knot invention.

That early in the morning no one was about. I grabbed the case, sank to the bottom, and flippered over to Octo's den. Starting to open the dynamite case, Octo greeted me with tentacles roaming all over me and the case. I apologized to Octo that I didn't have crab. *But I brought you a surprise that might blow your mind.*

I opened the case and proceeded to load the dynamite into his den. Octo stayed by me as if curious what I was about. I packed three-fourths of the den with dynamite, leaving little room for Octo. I saved out one stick for the primer insertion. I poked a hole big enough to insert the primer with the wires attached. Then I made sure the primer was embedded deep in the pile of dynamite, taping both wires so they could not touch.

Then I backed off to admire my work. *Looks good,* I concluded. The hole in the base of the rock did not leave much thickness to the outside walls; if the blast didn't shatter the rock, it would definitely knock it over. I returned to my truck and planned to come back next morning. I said a prayer for Octo, that he'd survive the night with all that dynamite.

The next morning, Sunday, I arrived with my roll of wire. It was quite a distance to the rock from the front of the dock. I jumped in and swam out to visit Octo—and attach the wires. Octo had gone! I glanced about hopefully, but suddenly he showed up looking for a crab handout. *Sorry, buddy no crab today.* He was all over me. I had to take off my gloves to attach the wires, and Octo grabbed one to see if he could eat it. Not edible, the glove started to float away. I was glad to get it back. Didn't want to be underwater too long without a glove. The wires properly secured, I walked backwards on the bottom unrolling the coil of wire. I had to hurry because I didn't know how long the dynamite would remain stable underwater. Octo followed me all the way to the dock. I climbed up the ladder and dropped my tank and weight belt and went to the truck to get battery. Returning, I expected to see Octo climbing the ladder looking for breakfast. It was almost 4:00 a.m. I went over to the live tank and grabbed a crab and climbed down the ladder. To my relief, there was Octo! Tossing the crab well up under the dock almost out of the water, Octo went after it. As fast as I could, I raced back up onto the dock, hoping Octo would not immediately take his breakfast back to his den.

Touching the two wires to the battery, one to positive, one to negative, I watched a monumental column of water erupt from the surface. The explosion was muffled by the water, but it was still pretty loud—luckily not enough to blow out any windows.

A few moments later, sculpin and other fish appeared floating, but the current quickly took them away. I didn't see Octo floating on the surface! He had been a long way from the den. I was sure he found other digs. I was just happy the dynamite didn't go off before I was ready!

Leaping into my truck, I peeled out of there before anyone came around wondering what the noise was. Sunday morning had been ideal. If anyone looked out toward Near Island, they might see some very murky water and a few dead fish. Other than that, no evidence.

The next morning at oh-dark-thirty, I swam out to the location of the rock. It was gone. A good-sized hole was all that was left. It must have shattered into a million pieces.

I love it when a plan comes together. Especially my plan.

Dynamite

Something in the water, what could it be
A boatload of crab coming in from the sea
A bump on the way into the dock
Out there? Could it possibly be a rock?
I better dive in and have a look-see
There is a rock out there solid as can be
There is something moving underneath
It is an octopus, a big one in its lair
You gotta go, Octo, another den to find
I have a surprise that might blow your mind

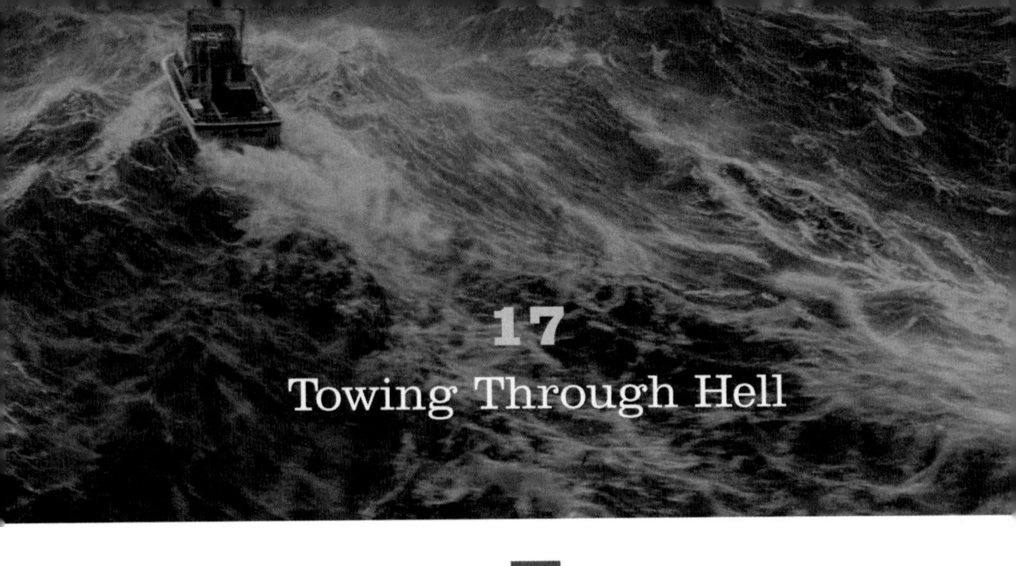

17
Towing Through Hell

The last place you would want to be was in a winter storm in the Strait of Georgia off Vancouver Island. (I was soon to be on a trip that only added to other questionable thoughts I was having about being on boats.)

1962. Kodiak, Alaska. The salmon season had closed up for the year. I was walking down the Alaska Packers cannery float doing a personal survey of the activities of the day. A small crew nearby loaded boxes onto a big 105-foot power scow with the name *Balena* painted on her bow. I was not necessarily looking for a job, but it seemed to me like this operation could use some help. The guy giving orders appeared to be the captain in charge of this large chunk of wood. I asked him if he could use some help.

The man looked at me. "Can you read a compass?"

I replied, "Yes I can."

"Let's find out. Follow me," he called back.

The captain introduced himself as Cliff Holliver. We climbed up into the wheelhouse and walked over to the compass. I stood up to the helm while Cliff gave me compass points—not compass degrees. He started by asking me to show him the course you would steer east by a quarter north, then south by three-quarters west, and then a few more. Finally he said, "You are the only guy I have met that knew all the points of a compass. If you want a job, you can sail with me as the first mate." Lucky for me, when I was in the Sea Scouts we had to know all the points of the compass for the navigating merit badge.

I went back to my boarding house room and gathered my sailing stuff and some extra clothes and boarded the *Balena*.

The loading program had been short a few hands until I'd joined the crew. Then I noticed a rugged-looking man, possibly Sun'aq tribe, walking along the dock. He asked if we needed more help. I called out, "Come aboard." He had a little canvas bag and the clothes on his back. I asked him where his gear was, and he said, "This is it." His name was Eddie Topkok, from Teller, Alaska. He told me about his family, which had the largest reindeer herd in that part of the country. Then he told me his story. The previous winter the herd got scattered in a storm and blizzard that lasted for days. He had spent a lot of time rounding up the last of them near Nome. Having no clue how to get them back home, he found a buyer in Nome and sold the entire herd. Exhausted, sad about having to sell the family herd, he caught a plane to Fairbanks, got drunk, and stayed drunk. The money that was supposed to go to the family was gone. How he managed to get to Kodiak, he didn't seem to remember. He was sobering up and obviously in pain. I asked him what was in the canvas bag. He opened it up. It was full of ivory and carving tools. There were no personal hygiene kit or clothes. "Okay," was all I could think to say. Now we had a full crew.

After supper, we headed out from Kodiak for Larson Bay on the other side of the island with 250 tons of canned salmon on board. I had some extra clothes that I gave Eddie. He was sweating booze loading that 250 tons of salmon. It took him a few days to get back in condition, but he pulled himself together. At Larson Bay we took on a 100-foot barge loaded with a generator and other equipment headed south for repairs for the next season.

After we had everything aboard and secured with chain binders, and the tow properly set for sea, with the captain's wife as cook, we were ready to head south. Not long underway I discovered the captain was an alcoholic. It appeared that his other first mate was a bottle of Jack Daniels.

Wheel watch on a boat or ship is usually four hours, and if a large crew maybe three. We left Larson Bay as the sun was setting, and I was on wheel watch from that first evening until 6:00 the next morning. *Ten-hours!* Cliff managed to do okay during the day but, by the time evening rolled around, he was incapacitated. Eddie stood wheel watches with me and told stories of living and hunting in the Arctic. His stories kept me awake. He carved ivory seals, walrus, whales, and other trinkets while we sailed south. I had an 8mm movie camera, and I took some movies of Eddie carving a walrus. It took him 25 minutes. This guy is incredible!

After a few days we entered Johnstone Strait, at the north end of Vancouver Island, and cruised down to Chatham Point, then to Seymore Narrows. We rounded Cape Mudge into less protected waters, a little north of the Strait of Georgia, and the wind hit us hard and the swells caused our scow to jump off of one big wave and crash into the next one, jarring the teeth. After the third crash, Cliff showed up in the wheelhouse to see what had thrown him out of his bunk.

In the small galley, the refrigerator doors flew open, and everything in the refrigerator came out, crashing to the deck. Macaroni salad, ham hocks and beans, mayonnaise, ketchup! With each dive into another wave, food slid fore to aft and port to starboard. I managed to get the refrigerator doors tied shut, but standing up in the galley was like dancing the light fantastic. I almost made it without hitting the deck, but the law of averages won. Cliff took the wheel. That made me happy. I have never seen swells like this traveling the inside waters of Canada. They were monstrous, and the *Balena* has a blunt bow that made it feel like we are hitting a rock wall!

We made it as far as the north end of Texada Island and held position in its lee. Cliff held her steady and yelled for Eddie and me to go forward and drop anchor. Seeing as there was no one for me to delegate the job to, I went with Eddie. We donned rain gear, headed out the door, and almost got blown off the deck. The cable attached alongside the railing forward was our lifeline. It blew so hard I had to scream in Eddie's ear so he could hear me. Together we lifted the dog out of its slot, turned the wheel holding brakes on the winch, and let the anchor go.

The wind drove us back, so no need for Cliff to reverse the engines. Our tow, that 100-foot barge, also helped pull us back. The anchor held—*so far!* I dogged the anchor and tightened the brake.

Back in the wheelhouse, we watched the radar to see if we continued to hold position. We watched. Waited. Then, we started to drift!

The wind and the barge were too much for the selected anchorage. We were dragging our anchor. Cliff ordered us to wind in the tow line and get that barge as close as possible to the *Balena*. The barge was acting like a wind sail.

Holding us steady with both engines forward, winding in the towline was not a simple task. The barge swung back and forth snapping the towing hawser with such force it bent the fairlead on the winch. We had to time the slack periods to winch it in a little at a time.

Finally, the barge was close enough to the stern of the *Balena* that we could secure the winch. Then back to the bow to wind up the anchor chain. Anchor up, it was back to the wheelhouse.

The radio station from local transmissions said the wind was blowing the roofs off houses and toppling trees, estimated at 120–150 miles per hour. Cliff got the bow of the *Balena* as close in as he could without grounding it. Once again, Eddie and I headed forward in the screaming wind. We had to hang on tight to everything or get blown overboard. We dropped the anchor and let out all the chain and some of the wire. We appeared to be holding in place.

Again, back in the wheelhouse, all eyes were glued to the radar. We held. Then we didn't.

The boat started drifting backwards. Cliff put the vessel in gear forward to try and reset it. Again, forward, Eddie and I hauled in the anchor. I signaled Cliff to go ahead, and he moved us east across the top of Texada Island where we dropped the anchor.

Impossibly, winds were picking up even more. The barge, close to the stern, leaped up and down, snapping the tow line so hard we thought the it was going to pull the towing winch right off the deck. The *Balena* was being dragged astern faster and faster, the anchor again not holding.

For the sixth time, maybe tenth time, I'd lost count, Eddie and I made our way forward to the anchor winch. The dog had snapped off. The wire was gone.

I passed the bad news to Cliff. Told him we better let some line out on the barge. We had no anchor. All we could do now was head out into the strait and plow our way south. Back on the stern, I let the tow line out about 200 feet. We still had the barge.

Sailing south down the turbulent and raging Strait of Georgia, Eddie stayed tow watch. I helped Cliff's wife clean up the mess in the galley.

Early morning, rounding Point Roberts into Boundary Bay, we tied up at the Alaska Packers dock in Blaine, Washington. We saw dock workers picking up pieces of cannery roof and other wind-blown debris. When they saw us pull in, they couldn't believe we had come down through the straits in that storm. *We had no choice. Davey Jones stole our anchor.*

The Columbus Day Storm of 1962 (also known as the Big Blow, and originally as Typhoon Freda) was a Pacific Northwest windstorm that struck the West Coast of Canada and the Pacific Northwest coast. It was a benchmark of extratropical wind storms in the 20th century. It snapped off thousands of trees all up and down the west coast and caused millions of dollars in damage.

Just another trip to talk about.

Towing Through Hell

A job not needed just checking the float
I see a small crew is loading a boat
A big boat named *Balena*, it's a power scow
Stopped to talk to the Captain, he says well now
You looking for a job? I need a mate
To help me sail south and I can't be late
I climbed aboard wondering what's in store
We know not what's next and will wonder no more

18
Dead in the Water

"Jerry. This is United States Coast Guard, Kodiak. We have a distress call from Taiyo Fisheries Company, Tokyo, informing us one of their fishing vessels is in distress in the Gulf of Alaska southeast from Kodiak Island.

"They are dead in the water. The ship has the trawl net wrapped up in their prop and are requesting an assist. They are outside 12-mile limit, and we do not have a vessel currently available. We have contacted Kodiak Airways about a chopper, and they have one available, if you can use it to get to them."

That beautiful summer day, I agreed to fly out to the disabled ship and try to remove the trawl net from the prop. I called Kodiak Airways, talked with Bob Hall. I said I'd be there in half an hour. Asked to have Ron Mosgood warm a unit up. Ron and I had many hours flying in and around Kodiak Island. We also covered the Aleutian Islands doing dive jobs. I'd surveyed vessels on the bottom, about to be on the bottom, and some stuck on the rocks never to float again. Ron had been a general's pilot during the Vietnam War. His expertise was unparalleled in maneuvering that small Bell Jet Helicopter. I would fly to hell and back if he were the pilot.

I had brought my own modified, full custom rebuilt, three-eighths-inch-thick wet suit, along with flippers and dive tank. We loaded them in the chopper and checked all the other gear that might be needed for the job. Two knives: one with a chisel end and razor-sharp cutting edge made from a truck leaf spring and hardened equal to schedule 8 steel; the other with a serrated edge for cutting through most nylon or propylene lines, or a trawl net wrapped around a prop shaft. Face mask, regulator, and weight belt with attached clasp for holding my tools completed the kit. While diving at sea you *did not* want to drop a tool, because it would be gone! If you needed that particular tool to do the job at hand, the job was over, done or not; no pay for job failure regardless of the circumstances.

I was ready, and Ron was ready, and we were off. The weather looked ideal, visibility superb. About an hour out we easily spotted the Japanese vessel in distress. She was indeed dead in the water.

Along the way, we passed a number of other fishing vessels active in the area. Before the 200-mile international limit went into effect, foreign fleets were a constant sight just outside of the U.S. coastal waters' 12-mile limit. We circled the Japanese ship—her entire crew on deck waving at us. She was clearly in trouble, rolling helplessly with the ocean swell.

I got into my gear, not a simple task in the back seat of a small helicopter. I told Ron I was ready, and he hovered close to the ship about 25–30 feet above the ocean surface. Attaching the regulator to the air tank is standard procedure. Remembering to turn on the air valve that supplies air to the regulator is critical. Once I forgot to do that; fortunately, I was diving with my partner who turned it on after we surfaced from the jump.

Sliding the chopper door open, I climbed out on the runner, put the mouthpiece regulator between my teeth, looked down at the crew on the deck of the ship all with their mouths hanging agape, grabbed a tight grip on my face mask, and jumped. I surfaced and waved to Ron, then watched the small Bell helicopter turn off and head back to Kodiak. I was on my own, in the Gulf of Alaska, completely out of sight of land. Adrenaline surged throughout my body—which, I reminded myself, is why I do this. *I love it!*

Signaling the ship's crew hanging over the stern railing, I dived under the stern and got to work. The vessel rolled in the swell, but not seriously enough to obstruct my efforts to evaluate the damage. Underwater visibility was excellent and I saw the problem instantly. The cod end of the net was wrapped around the wheel (prop) so tight it broke the rib lines and ripped the cod end from the throat of the net. Killed the engine's rotation. They would still have their engine, but no power to the prop.

The rest of the net must be on deck or the reel. It was a lucky break for me, as all that was required would be to unwind the net from the prop. More than likely, they got tangled when they were setting the net. How this happened is kind of strange because when setting the net, the vessel should be heading forward; the prop wash would force the net out away from the ship. I reckon I had better things to do than trying to figure out how they got tangled.

I noticed that this cod-end still had fish stuck in the webbing. It was heavier than I thought and unwinding it required some additional effort just to get it over the top of the prop. I managed to get the first wrap over, but the weight of that cod end hanging straight down needed to be lifted up and over. I should have called Marion Parker, my dive partner at Aleutian Divers.

Too late for that. Sometimes I could be over-optimistic, certain I was superhuman.

I surfaced and managed to convey to the crew that I needed a line to tie on the net. Clearly no one on board could speak English, and I couldn't speak Japanese. But sign language worked! They got me the end of a line. Underwater again, I tied the line on the loose end of the net that was hanging down, then surfaced and waved to them to pull on the line carefully. Back below, I managed to get the end over the prop, pulled it aft, and got it clear. Up on deck, they continued to pull, and as the end cleared the surface of the water I hung on.

The cod end of the net, along with me, was dragged up the stern ramp.

The chief engineer made it clear with lots of hand gestures he wanted to know how the prop looked, if there was any damage. I gestured back all was okay, and added, "*Ichiban*," which I believed meant "number one" or "good."

They seemed to be amazed at my jump into the sea, expressing their appreciation with hand signals. The captain pointed towards Kodiak, and shook his head up and down, which I assumed meant he knew I needed to get back to Kodiak. I did likewise, signifying that I agreed.

The crew brought me tea laced with enough sugar to float a spoon. I said, "*Watashi arigato*." I knew that meant "thank you."

Shortly after finishing my tea, a small Coast Guard vessel came alongside the Japanese ship. The captain once again was bowing and shaking my hand, quite obviously grateful for me getting his ship back in action.

I gathered my face mask and regulator and jumped overboard. The Coast Guard picked me out of the water and returned me to Kodiak.

This was the beginning of many such adventures flying into the Gulf of Alaska, jumping out of a helicopter, removing lines and nets from Japanese fishing vessels. The next time out there, I called Marion to accompany me, so we both could get an adrenaline rush.

Dead in the Water

A foreign fishing vessel fifteen miles offshore
A fishing net in the wheel and can move no more
A radio call goes out, anyone have a diver aboard ship
Answer comes back, Kodiak has one but it's long off
A helicopter is on its way and hope you are ready to pay
A diver jumps out into the sea and dives under the stern
A thought comes to mind, a lot of money he will earn
A big net wrapped up tight, he needs lots of slack
After surfacing he wonders "How am I gonna get back?"

19
Save the *Naknek*

Yippee! Spring time in Kodiak, Alaska. The snow melt runs muddy in the streets, winter's accumulation of doggie doo is exposed, snow-hidden garbage arises as if from the grave, and first rains assist in the meltdown.

We needed the rain. It helped wash the winter's accumulation into the sea. Many advantages existed however, one being with the doggie doo; the mud exposed in your line of sight meant you could sidestep it instead of scraping it off your boots later before you entered a house. In the streets, only boots were worn this time of year. In Kodiak as well as other Alaskan communities there was a standing rule: no one ever entered your house with boots or shoes, regardless of the time of year.

Kodiak Island had a few villages and numerous harbors, bays, inlets, and rivers—the only access in most cases being by air or boat. This is where I lived and worked, much of the time underwater, and very often taking jobs that others refused or were unqualified to do. A lot of jobs, whether coastal or out in the Gulf of Alaska, required flying to various locations in big planes, little planes, float planes, or jet helicopters.

In the spring the salmon canneries prepared for the summer runs of salmon, and the only way to transport equipment and supplies to remote canneries was by boat. Most canneries had their own fleet of salmon tenders. These tender vessels cruised around to the areas where the salmon trawlers fished and then offloaded their catch onto the tenders, which in turn delivered the salmon to their specific cannery for processing. Most of the old wooden tenders, or power scows, averaged 85 feet in length and were 30 feet wide, while a few were 105 feet in length. They had a house aft with an open forward deck, two diesel engines, and twin screws—commonly known as props or wheels. These boats were the workhorses of the salmon seasons, hauling everything except the cannery crews to processing plants located all over Alaska.

At their company's docks in and around Seattle, each tender's crew loaded and secured with chains and load binders their equipment and supplies for the upcoming salmon season. These boat captains had many years of experience loading tenders and traveling to and from Alaska. They knew the tides, depths, and shipping lanes north and south, memorized the routes, markers, aids, and entrance lights, and had learned the perils that lurked in the dark upon and below the sea.

Departing the Seattle area loaded to the waterline (a few below), the tenders traveled north through the inside passage of British Columbia, then Southeast Alaska, trying their best to stay out of the weather and the rolling seas of the North Pacific. For those who had to travel as far as the Bering Sea and Bristol Bay, they'd leave early April hoping for smoother sailing. Leaving the Inside Passage of Southeast Alaska out Cross Sound into the Gulf of Alaska, the ocean swells could shift cargo and inundate decks with violent green water and foaming seas. (Once in a while steaming up Icy Strait, out Cross Sound, and into the Gulf, one can catch a glimpse of a line in the sea shimmering in brief sunlight where green water turns to blue.)

Sailing north, a tender captain usually navigated close in to shore past Yakutat, and then, weather permitting, cut across the southern tip of Kodiak Island. In bad weather it was often safer to head north around Kodiak through Shelikof Strait to Unimak and False Pass, finally sailing up the northern coast of the Alaska Peninsula to Bristol Bay.

Cargo carried by these company boats was extremely valuable, not only due to its cost but because, without the supplies required to operate for the coming season, they would not be able to start on time or maybe not at all.

Early one spring the New England Fish company's tender, M/V *Naknek*, was on its way to Bristol Bay loaded with cannery equipment and supplies. Stormy weather had forced its course north up the southeast side of Kodiak Island, then west through Shelikof Strait to Unimak Island and False Pass. A storm had been lashing Kodiak Island for several days. The few boats caught out in the weather sought shelter in any bay or the lee of any island they could find. Rainfall was record-breaking, and it always rained sideways in Kodiak, with cloud cover down to the water. It felt like you were being pelted with a fusillade of lead BBs. Such conditions were called "zero visibility." No planes flew in such weather, no boats fished.

As for me, given those conditions, life was on slow. I was dry, warm, and comfortable, with no immediate diving projects on my calendar. However, underwater jobs were never concerned with dry or wet weather, hot or cold, wind or no wind.

Well, I guess I was just too comfortable, because the phone rang and it was Kodiak Airways informing me that the Coast Guard had called them about flying a helicopter—*in this weather!*—across the island to Ugak Bay. They did not have a chopper on the base at that time, and could not get a boat around there in time to save a distressed vessel from certain death on a pile of rocks. "What's the problem with the vessel that you needed a diver?" I asked. They said, "Hang up and I'll call you back with more information." So I hung up the phone and thought, maybe I had better start gathering my dive gear in case I need to go swimming.

Ten minutes later the Coast Guard called me back with the details. A vessel, the power scow *Naknek*, had sought shelter from the storm in Ugak Bay. Because of the limited visibility the vessel ran through a Dungeness crab fisherman's string of gear and became disabled. Crab lines with buoys attached had wrapped both props tight and killed their two main engines. They seemed unable to drop anchor and were drifting into the beach. It sounded to me like the anchor winch was probably operated from the power-take-off (known as the PTO) mounted to the main engine. No main engine, no anchor winch. They were dead in the water, drifting towards the rocks, at the mercy of wind and swell!

As soon as I got on the line with the Coast Guard, Bob Hall of Kodiak Airways called. He already had Ron Mosgood warming up the chopper. I'd better hurry down to the landing. Kodiak Airways was located right downtown, not far from me. I had already powdered my wet suit and slipped into it. At the Kodiak Airways landing pad, ready to go, I loaded all my gear into the rear door of the chopper. Two dive tanks, regulators, fins, face mask, plus two pair of neoprene gloves, I climbed in the co-pilot's door and strapped myself in.

Ron said, "I hope you're ready for this trip, because it is going to be rough."

I gave him my same old reply when anyone asked me that: "I was born ready."

We left the landing pad and pitched and bounced our way south, skimming the surface of the water because of the low ceiling, searching for a power scow in distress. Time was of the essence!

A nasty day, I mused, for flying in anything other than a 747 at 37,000 feet.

Ron and I had clocked many hours together in the small sleek Bell helicopter. He was an exceptional pilot, and I never gave a second thought to my safety regardless of the conditions. He had transported me to numerous dive sites, including the deep blue waters of the Gulf of Alaska.

We crossed over Middle Bay and up into the head of Kalsin Bay, then followed the American River through the pass to Ugak Bay. Visibility was just about zero, and the rain hitting the windscreen sounded like bullets. We were ground-hopping and scaring the feathers off the slow-moving ptarmigan. We cruised up Ugak Bay, flying through fog, wind, and rain at about 50 feet off the water. We passed below an eagle that was clinging to a weather-beaten tree branch on a rock sticking out of a cliff, and he gazed down at us with a bewildered look and opened his beak as if to say, "What?"

When we came upon her, the *Naknek*, an overloaded power scow, was rolling broadside on the swell drifting right up into Saltry Cove, not a good place to be with any type of floating equipment. There was no beach visible and all we could see were rocks—big rocks!

We circled around the boat a couple times to make certain she was the M/V *Naknek*. I crawled into the back of the chopper and donned my tank and gear. I never used a buoyancy compensator (BC), so I had a lot more maneuverability. I rechecked everything before I opened the door and stepped out on the runner. I had told Ron to hover about 30 to 40 feet off the water and upwind. Grabbing my face mask and regulator with both hands, I jumped. (If I lost my regulator or face plate, I'd be out of business and so would the boat.)

I hit the water straight with all necessary gear intact. Breaking the surface to get my bearings, I swam over to the boat through wind-swept chop and swell. Near the stern of the power scow, I hollered up to the anxious crew to secure a ladder over the side. "I'll be right back," I yelled.

Down beneath the stern the scene was awesome. The twin props were completely covered by a mass of line wrapped around each wheel. The port wheel had a crab pot wrapped around it. Fortunately, the crab pot was the last thing to get caught in the wheel, so I had easy access to the iron bars. But I couldn't move the pot, not even a jiggle, it was wrapped so tight, and the only way out was a hack saw.

I surfaced again and called to the crew to get me two hacksaws and all the blades they could find. Hacksaw blades could snap with little effort. These boys were fast! They disappeared like smoke in a hurricane and returned moments later with a handful of tools. I grabbed a saw and dove down to the wheels.

The boat was bouncing up and down in the swell, and it was a test to see if I could hold on and saw at the same time. Prior to my submerging, I saw that we were about 100 yards from the beach—and the rocks!

I hacked my way through the iron bars of the pot, probably broke some record for sawing up a crab pot with a hacksaw. I was sawing so fast I was surprised that I wasn't generating steam. Having cut through enough bars, by putting both feet against the prop and pulling with both hands I ripped the remaining iron bars off the prop blades. Back on the surface, I handed a crew member the saw, turned upside down, and headed back to cut away the lines and buoys. I could see that the rocky bottom now appeared to be no more than 20 feet from the boat's keel. The clock was ticking!

I always carried my big custom knife made from a truck spring. It was razor sharp, very heavy, and had a flat edge chisel on the end of the blade. I hacked away and cut line with every bit of speed I could muster until all the line was out of the props. Elapsed time: 20 minutes.

The scow was at most about 50 yards from the beach. I felt something hit my flipper. The rocks on the bottom were within six feet of the hull as the boat slid to the bottom of a swell. It was a bit nerve-wracking swimming between the bottom of the boat and the rocks. Good thing I'm fearless, I told myself.

Once again on the surface, I hollered to the crew, "Start your mains!"

One deck hand disappeared like a bolt of lightning. I grabbed the ladder, climb up to the aft deck, was grabbed and lifted clear onto the deck. As the engines growled to life, the reduction gear was engaged and prop wash moved us slowly away from the beach.

I have never seen three happier faces on men who a half-hour before had doubts about their boat and their lives. The *Naknek* was about as close as a boat can get to the rocks and survive. Lots of hand-shaking. For a minute I thought they were going to kiss me.

The captain laughed and asked me, "What am I going to do with you?"

I said, "See that chopper over there, above the rocks out by the head of the bay?"

He acknowledged that, by God, there was a helicopter sitting there.

I told him to head out of the bay until he was adjacent to the chopper then turn in toward the beach. "I'll be up on the bow, and when I raise my hand, you start backing down and I'll jump off and swim ashore through the surf and breakers from there."

He asked me if I was crazy, and I replied "Absolutely. Do you think I would be out here if I wasn't?"

The captain couldn't thank me enough and was certain I was going to get myself killed trying to get ashore through those breakers. I told him I didn't want to ride with him into Kodiak, because I would get seasick and I preferred chancing the breakers to being seasick. Actually, I had already picked a spot that appeared to be reasonably free of rocks and less surf to crash through.

After that little episode, I thought to myself, so much for my vast experience and wisdom getting through the raging surf unscathed. My wet suit suffered more than I did. The suit could be easily repaired, my body might require a little more time.

Ron was waiting patiently on his little knoll barely large enough to hold his machine. I could see the chopper rocking from the wind. He saw me hit the water and cranked up the screaming windmill so we could lift off into the darkening sky as soon as I tumbled and crawled my way through the breakers, climbed up over the rocks, then clawed my way up the steep muddy bank to the chopper.

Diving gear is easily carried in the water, but on land, climbing hills and crawling in mud with an air tank, weight belt, and flippers, it's a different story! I was exhausted by the time I reached the chopper. It was raining with such violence, it washed all the mud from the front of my wet suit. Ron was mighty particular about the inside of his chopper. Seawater dripping was okay, but mud was not.

I took off my tank and weight belt, threw them in the back, tossed my flippers in, and then climbed into the co-pilot's seat. Away we went.

The storm had not abated and the ceiling appeared to be lower than when we arrived. So, we scattered water surface birds and ground-dwelling wildlife all the way back to the landing pad in Kodiak. I patted myself on the back knowing I had just saved the New England Fish Company a half a million dollars or more. And I made three men extremely happy and prodigiously grateful.

That felt good.

The Coast Guard Station Commander called and thanked me for my heroics.

Ah shucks—just another day in the life of a working diver.

Save the *Naknek*

Stormy weather too much for a loaded boat
Has to find a safe anchorage and stay afloat
They didn't see the crab buoys and pots
A string of crab gear gets into the props
Kills both engines as it heads for the rocks
Any chance someone can help us
Probably not, it's blowing sixty plus

20
AK-47

At our seafood-integrated company, SeaWest Industries, we were always looking for opportunities to expand operations and explore diverse avenues of financial success. It meant we would sometimes travel outside of our regular operating areas of Alaska and Washington.

As Vice President of Operations, I was elected to search out such opportunities. Our connections with some Japanese companies gave us a lead to operations in Chile that we were then interested in checking out. One of the places I visited was the city of Punta Arenas, located on the Strait of Magellan on the southern tip of Chile. Our company made some calls and arranged for me to meet a man there who had a King crab operation.

On the plane trip south, it occurred to me I hadn't thought through the language situation. Not even slightly conversant in Spanish, I wondered how I was going get around, let alone negotiate a contract. The last person off the plane, I glanced through the Plexiglas wall separating the baggage area and noticed someone who appeared to be waving to me. There was no one directly behind me so I walked around the barrier, and there stood Fumio, a Japanese man that we had done business with in Dutch Harbor. I couldn't believe it! From the top of the planet to the bottom of the planet, I meet the same guy.

"What are you doing here?" I asked.

He replied with a smile, "Probably the same thing you are." He was there looking to buy crab for his Japanese company.

At the car rental agency, I ran into some Texans who were in

Chile to work on oil wells. The rental agent was talking to them in perfect English.

After the Texans had finished, I got up to the desk and asked the young man with "Carlos" on his name tag, where he learned to speak English so well?

Carlos replied, "I was an exchange student living and going to school in Detroit."

I then asked, "How much are you making here renting cars?"

"About one hundred eighty dollars a month American."

I was in dire need of an interpreter, so I suggested to Carlos if he would like to work for me, I would pay him a thousand a month. He jumped over the counter, and threw the keys he held in his hand to the other guy behind the counter, and told him, "I quit."

Carlos was quick to grasp the situation, and with his help, I made a deal with a crab plant owner and settled in to start production. We had to wait for a few days before the boats arrived to deliver the King crab, which the locals called Centolla

While we were waiting for a delivery that was several days out, I decided to drive to Rio Gallegos, which had a large harbor, located on the southern coast of Argentina across the lower Andes Mountains. I thought there must be crab operations or other possibilities located there.

I rented Carlos' dad's pickup truck, and Carlos and I took off for Argentina, north on Highway 9 to Morro Chico, then across the border into Argentina. We had great weather driving through a countryside of abundant green grass, white-face cattle, and thousands of sheep. We saw a gaucho on a horse on a hill. Other than the animals and this lone cowboy, the land was empty, no farmhouses, buildings, barns, power poles, nothing. Occasionally, we drove over large splotches of white on the gravel road, which I later learned was the remains of roadkill. Sheep would stray outside their fenced pastures and be run over by the big diesel trucks hauling trailers loaded with cattle and sheep at 70 miles an hour.

After a few hours, we came to a guard station out in the middle of nowhere with a gate across the road. As we came, a guard stepped out carrying an AK-47. The guard approached and motioned for us to get out. I opened the driver's door, while Carlos asked him what he wanted. The guard walked up to me, stuck the barrel of his rifle in my chest, and demanded my passport. I gave him the passport, and he handed it to another guy who had come out of the station.

"Ah-hah," he said, "*Americano.*"

Carlos said something to them in rapid Spanish.

The guard pushed his rifle in my chest again. "American *dinero.*"

I said, "No American dinero. Solo Chilean pesos." I kept my hands where he could see them. Moving very slowly, I reached into a pocket and pulled out some Chilean bills. Then I reached into my other pockets and turned them inside out. I offered him the few pesos I had. I hoped they didn't find out about the twenty 100 American dollar bills in my boots.

With one hand, the guard grabbed the pesos from me and put them in his pocket, never taking the rifle from my chest.

Carlos continued answering lots of questions, until they took him inside the building.

It was 1982. The timing wasn't the best. Argentina wanted America to back them up right after their invasion of the Falkland Islands. America refused. The Argentines did not like Americans. The guard continued to hold me at gun-point until Carlos finally came out of the building with our passports. The second guard came out with Carlos, said something to the gun guy, who finally lowered his AK-47.

Back in the truck. They lifted the gate and let us through. Carlos told me the only reason they let us pass was that we were to deliver a letter and a small package to the second guard's house in Rio Gallegos, and then his wife would give us a package to bring to him upon our return. Carlos also told the head guy that we were looking for a business venture in Argentina, and he said that, upon arrival in Rio Gallegos, we were to report to the police station.

We had a helluva time finding the house where we were to deliver the package. When we did, the guard's wife gave Carlos the parcel we would deliver to the husband on our return.

At the police station, they wanted to know why it had taken us so long to check in with them; we hadn't known they'd gotten a call from the guard station that we were coming. Anyway, we were checked out, passports reviewed, questions answered. They finally let us go to a hotel, but instructed us to inform the hotel to call the police station and report our arrival. We checked into the hotel, got settled, and then went to find some food.

I pulled some small denomination money from a boot and away we went.

We found a nearby restaurant and ordered two fillet mignon dinners and a bottle of red wine. The waitress brought each of us a salad and a plate with two medallions of beef that I swear you could cut with a fork. That was followed by a dessert of pie à la mode. Our check was the equivalent of $4 American. Carlos paid with Chilean pesos. I gave the waitress an American $5 tip, and I thought she was going to kiss me. She bowed, said over and over, "*¡Gracias, gracias, señor!*"

There was an 8:00 p.m. curfew, and when we got back to our room, metal shutters were automatically lowered from the outside to cover the windows. I thought, if there was a hotel fire in the hallway, we would have no way out.

Checking out in the morning, I gave the manager a $100 bill for the rooms and he gave me an Argentine 500,000 peso bill. I had no idea what it was worth.

I drove around until we found the boat harbor. It was empty. Not a single boat anywhere. I got out to take a picture. A soldier appeared out of nowhere. He had another replica of what I had stuck in my chest the day before. He shouted, "No photographica!" I said "okay" in sign language, then asked, "*Habla usted ingles?*" He shook his head no. I verbally told him what I thought—in English—then jumped in the truck and drove a little farther down, got out, and took a picture of a beautiful, empty boat harbor. But there were too many soldiers with guns around. I noticed huge signs on the sides of buildings that read "If you want freedom vote *communista*." I told Carlos we were getting outta here!

I drove off south instead of the way we had come, taking an alternate route back to Punta Arenas via highway 255 along the shoreline by the Strait of Magellan. Carlos was shocked, and said we have to deliver the package to the guard station.

I said, "Give me the package."

Carlos handed it to me, and I threw it out the window.

Carlos gasped, saying, "What if they contact the guard station where we entered Argentina?"

I told him we would chance it.

At the customs station, Carlos took our passports inside, while I waited in the truck. A few minutes later he waved at me to come into the guard station. They looked at me to see if I matched the passport picture, then let me return to the truck, where I waited some more for Carlos. I started to worry we would be told to go back the way we had come—without the package that I had thrown out the window.

Finally, Carlos appeared with a big smile and got in the truck. They let us into Chile! It was like I was going home. A great relief!

Huge trucks going by us at 60 miles an hour threw rocks in all directions. All the trucks had heavy wire mesh attached from the front bumper up and over the windshield to protect them from cracks and breakage. Unfortunately, Carlos' pickup didn't have that protection. When we got back to Punta Arenas, I gave him enough money to get a new windshield.

AK-47

From Punta Arenas to Argentina across the pampas
A guard appears from nowhere to stop us
This is beginning to be no fun
As I am looking down the barrel of a gun

21 Puzzling Ice Dive

Kodiak, Alaska, like most Alaskan towns, gets cold in the winter. Unfortunately, winters have a habit of prolonging the anxiously awaited warmth of spring rains. Usually coastal winters are not as severe as the more northern reaches of the mainland, but bad enough to freeze pipes that are left unprotected, and they can even freeze up the water supply to town. The reservoir for the city is situated behind the town on the road to Pillar Mountain, and it is fed by hillside runoff and springs. The main spring that feeds the reservoir is not a rushing water creek in the winter, but it does continue to feed the small, if somewhat inadequate, Kodiak reservoir.

Several canneries in this small fishing village depend on the city to provide large quantities of fresh water for their processing procedures. Extended periods of freezing temperatures can cause the reservoir water level to decline, as snow in the hills doesn't melt and the spring flow doesn't maintain the water level required to keep the canneries operating.

One winter, below freezing temperatures kicked off right at the beginning of the winter solstice, December 21. The Kodiak reservoir's water level dropped lower and lower as the ice on the surface grew thicker and thicker. The actual level of the water was unknown because of the layer of ice. Then the unexpected happened. The city water quit flowing through the 16-inch feed line from the reservoir. With ice over 3 feet thick, there was no way to tell why the water had stopped, because this problem had never presented itself before. In prior years, the town never had so many processing plants, so it had never been a problem. Now it was a *huge* problem. Kodiak, Alaska, was entering winter without water!

The city maintenance crew sawed a big hole in the ice to see if they could determine why the water had quit flowing. But they couldn't see a thing just looking through that 3 feet of ice.

When my phone rang, I hoped it wasn't for a request to dive, because it was too cold out for anyone to be swimming, even in a good wet suit. Though I knew the water temperature was warmer than the air temperature, the initial shock of diving in felt equal to 220 volts, and not warm volts. That was what I feared the most, temperatures being in the teens.

I answered the phone. Herman Buekers, Kodiak's superintendent of the city's maintenance division, was frantic! He wanted me to dive under the reservoir ice sheet to see if I could determine the cause of the water stoppage. He was actually pleading with me, not asking. Of course, being Kodiak's only diver with compassion, fearlessness, and lots of experience, I agreed to dive through that hole in the 3-foot-thick ice.

Not a novice ice diver, I had worked on the water lines under the ice at Island Lake the previous winter. On one dive I had lost track of my entrance hole and I was diving without a tender. That was against all the rules for diving, especially ice diving. My diving partner had not been available, so I had decided to go it alone, figuring it would only take a few minutes to retrieve the frozen water line. Unable to find the entrance hole after circling a number of times, I took off my air tank and used it to break through the ice. Fortunately for me the ice had been only about 2 to 3 inches thick. I always learned the hard way.

I told Herman it would take me a little while to gather my gear.

I started up the truck and put the heater on full, then loaded the regulators and air tanks; that would keep them warm. Then I donned my custom made three-eighths-inch winter wet suit and loaded all the rest of the equipment in the truck. I drove up the hill to the reservoir and out on the ice. The city crew was already there, including, thank goodness, Skeezix Panamarof. Skeezix was a big guy, about three feet across the shoulders, and he could probably lift the front end of a truck. I would feel safe with my life line in his hands. Unfortunately, I did not have an experienced diver

tender. With all my weight belts, I would not use a buoyancy compensator, adjusting my own buoyancy by knowing the depth of my work and using the proper weight belt accordingly.

I had an instruction period with Skeezix and Herman. Skeezix would handle the life line, and I made certain he knew the signals, repeating each signal three times. To make it simple: one pull on the tag line meant haul back the slack; two pulls meant more slack and maintain tension at all times. There was no signal for stop as I knew the water in the reservoir was only about 20 ft deep.

It was so cold out, the water surface in the hole started freezing over. I securely attached the life line with my own knot, then attached my lightweight weight belt as fresh water has less buoyancy than seawater. I put on my air tank backpack with the regulator attached, which had been kept warm in the truck. Pulling down my face plate, I jumped into the ice hole. The water was extremely cold! I sank down about 15 feet when the regulator froze up.

I returned right to the surface. Skeezix reached down, grabbed me, and lifted me out of the water and onto the ice. The water on my suit immediately froze and cracked off as I moved.

Replacing the regulator with another hot one, I dove back in. After a few minutes, still not having found the problem, again my regulator froze. When the regulator freezes it remains open, so I got a mouthful of 2,500 pounds of air! I raced back to the ice hole and surfaced once again.

I told Skeezix I thought I had figured things out. When I dive, I've trained myself to breathe every 30 seconds and have been known to hold my breath up to 2 minutes in order to prolong the air in the tank. So, if I breathed normally and kept the warm air from my lungs going through the regulator, perhaps it wouldn't freeze up.

My next plunge into the depths of the reservoir was more successful. It's rather comical the difficulties I can overcome by using some common sense. I noticed the water level was about 4–5 inches from the bottom of the ice and little icicles were hanging down touching the water's surface. A very light current fed the reservoir and would not have been felt or noticed if it wasn't for the icicles moving around in the water. It was reasonably light and visibility was excellent. I could see clearly for about 15 feet. I found the problem as soon as I located the 16-inch pipe on the bottom that fed water to the town. There was a huge ball of ice sucked right down on top of the opening, and the pipe had no screen. It appeared the ice ball had formed from the accumulation of small icicles attaching together like a snowball as the current moved it along under the ice. When the ball of ice became about 2 feet in diameter and floated over the opening of the city water feed pipe, it then got sucked down by the vacuum created by the water flow from the reservoir.

Along the pipe and I could also see some seepage. I pulled my knife and poked at the ball of ice. I made a small groove in the bottom of the ball near the pipe opening. The suction was so powerful it pulled mud off the bottom some 18 inches below the opening. I could hear the suction and determined that it would not be a good idea to remove that ball of ice without a plan of escape. That suction could pull me into that pipe, and there would be no way I could pull myself free.

Having figured these things out, at that moment my regulator decided to freeze up again, so I returned to the surface.

I related my findings to the city crew and told them of my plan. I instructed Skeezix to hold the line firmly in his hand, so he could feel the slightest pull of my signal. I explained that I was going to try and dislodge the ball of ice by kicking it with my heel, and hopefully it would crumble from the sharp force of a high-powered kick. When I jerked that line, he was to start hauling as hard and fast as he could. I didn't want to end up as a permanent part of the city's water system.

Freezing in my wet suit, I was anxious to end this job and get home into a tub of hot water. My hands were numb, my head ached, my suit was a sheet of ice. I checked everything twice and walked over to the hole, made sure the knot was secure, asked Skeezix to repeat what I told him, then jumped back into the icy depths of the reservoir. I was positive this would work.

I descended to the pipe and the huge ice ball. Getting myself situated so my head was aimed back toward the hole, I checked to ascertain the life line had no obstruction, such as being tangled around my regulator or my tool belt. I then lay down on the bottom and raised my right flippered foot so it was exactly where I thought the kick would most likely shatter the ice ball. Holding the life line with both hands, I pulled back as far as my leg would go without breaking it loose from the hip joint and simultaneously kicked and jerked the life line. The ice ball crumbled, and I took off like I had a rocket attached to the other end of the life line. But it was just Skeezix doing exactly what I told him to do.

I saw the hole in the ice as I neared the surface at about ten knots. Then Skeezix reached down, grabbed my tank valve and regulator, jerked me free of the water, and plopped me standing straight up on the ice. This guy was one strong individual—the kind of person you want as a friend. Not only that, Skeezix was a nice person and always friendly.

I waited around for a little while to see if the kick did the trick. Herman went back to town to check that the water was indeed flowing. He returned with the good news that water was once again filling the town pipes. I was one cold, happy diver knowing I didn't have to jump back in the ice hole. Everyone called me a hero.

I just love this job.

Puzzling Ice Dive

Relaxing in my chair with a good book
Snow and ice through the window I look
A fire in the stove and all is nice
A call, the city has a problem under the ice
They ask if I will come to the reservoir
Any freezing cold days to work I abhor
No water to the town and fear arises
That hole in the ice is full of surprises

22
Rules, Rules, and Regulations

The Alaska seafood industry has had many changes in the past. Alaska seafood processors have adapted to new regulations. King crab fishing vessels have gone from small local converted salmon boats fishing with 30 small, round 125-pound crab pots to huge ships that haul and fish hundreds of big square 600- to 800-pound pots. Methods and rules have changed regularly. The small boats that used to anchor every night in a bay had low-density deck lights, if any at all, and navigated by compass and line of sight. Not so anymore.

Time marches on, and boats have continued to increase in size. New electronics were introduced that allowed the bigger and newer vessels to wander out of the sight of land. Pot restrictions were declared, as well as limits on how many crabs you could catch in any given area. Many regulations had to be accepted by the vessel owners. Then the U.S. Coast Guard started checking the fishing vessels. They wanted to determine if they all had the necessary gear for fighting fires, practiced man-overboard drills, maintained survival suits for every member of the crew and first aid kits, and kept updated life rafts and sailing charts.

Then someone developed quartz lights that were so powerful they would suck the pistons out of a standby generator. Installed on almost every boat, when turned on, the lights could shine a beam from Dutch Harbor to Japan. Every boat had to have these lights. Any boat harbor full of crab boats with their lights glaring could probably be seen from the International Space Station. Then came the ruling: *Do not have those blinding quartz lights turned on while traveling to and from your gear.*

Now back in the old days, we had to sail by chart courses, compass readings, current tables, tides, and absolutely no lights other than your running lights when underway. Any captain should be able to travel anywhere without lights, regardless of how big the license, or how big the ship or where that captain was sailing.

Rules are rules.

When any new regulations or area fishing borders and quotas are introduced to the fleet and the processors, I always seem to have a poem printed in one of the fishing magazines or fishermen's news either for or against the new rulings. It was usually against—just to prove a point. So many rules, I had to find a sense of humor about it, which resonates in the following poem.

Training to See at Sea

I got started kinda late; I guess it was back in '68
Late for me to be drawn to the Bering Sea
To the Aleutians and Dutch Harbor I came
To make it in this dangerous game

As the new man that I am you take what you can
A leaky boat in disrepair and a drunken crew that didn't care
The first trip nearly ended my time
When my arm was caught in a fast-moving line

I stayed on and finished the season
Then I quit for a very good reason
I needed a better boat for the coming year
One that I wouldn't fear

I got lucky and made it big and not dead
Even though every trip I'd dread
I quit from conscience appeal
But the memory goes and the scars do heal

So I said goodbye to my honey
Because I was out of money
It didn't take much time
And it was back to the Bering Sea in '69

The years passed and the boats increased in size
They continued to get bigger as if competing for a prize
Enough years on deck and pulling gear
I could be a skipper by the end of the year

But alas the U.S. Coast Guard changed the rules on me
Now I'm required to have a license to captain a ship at sea
So I enrolled in school but study was new to me
I studied long and hard with great difficulty

I entered every school and took every class
I hired tutors to guarantee I'd pass
I studied rules, inland, rivers and international
I took test after test and remained reasonably rational

I finished all the tests, I now have it made
My grades were at the top of the class
I knew I had made the grade
I went to survival school and firefighting, too

I tested all safety devices in the pool
I passed celestial and memorized every rule
I have an "A" rating in first aid and CPR
I can lower a lifeboat and raise a spar

Hell, I'm even certified for rapid radar
I now have licenses and certificates to cover the world
I am captain of any ship any ocean
But my dream is like an elixir potion

I want a giant King crab boat, new, all shiny and bright
One that has about 2 billion candle-power of fishing light
I'll be damned if I'll travel at night
Without a least 2 billion candle-power of lights

"What, me? Blinding others at sea?"
I suppose that's a possibility
But by God, I have to see
Where it is that I am going to be

PART
II

Platinum
CAPE NEWENHAM
TOGIAK BAY
Walrus Islands
Kulukak Bay
NUSHAGAK PEN
Clarks Point
KVICHAK BAY
NUSHAGAK BAY
Sterling Shoal
Egegik Bay
DANGER AREA 334.1280
(see note A)
B R I S T O L   B A Y
E   A
Ugashik Bay
Strogonof Pt
Port Heiden
Aniakchak Crater
A L A S K A   P E N I N S
Cape Seniavin
Cape Kutuzof
PORT MOLLER
Herendeen Bay
Cold Bay
Big Koniuji
Little Koniuji
Simeonof I
SHUMAGIN ISLANDS
SHUMAGIN BANK
AREA TO BE AVOIDED
SANAK
DAVIDSON BANK
ALEUTIAN TRENCH

23 Licensed to Shell

I received an invitation from one of our New York City seafood brokers to attend the grand opening of a lobster processing facility in Nassau, at the Atlantis Resort on Paradise Island in the Bahamas. It was a pretentious affair that certainly should have made the "Who's Who" section of the *New York Times*. There were several seafood brokers and suppliers, but only one that had a financial interest in investing in a lobster processing plant.

The first day, two owners of the newly christened lobster processing facility approached me. They asked if I could build a lobster catcher/processor. My standard reply, "No problem." I had never even cooked a lobster, but I certainly didn't reveal that, though. The seed had been planted, and it started to grow.

Something about creating a new system activated my inner design motivator. The seed didn't just start to grow, it was spreading like a forest fire in dry timber. I loved designing new systems, especially something with which I had no experience. Processing seafood is what I do. It should not be any different than processing other shellfish such as crabs, shrimp, scallops, clams, and oysters. Can I do this? *No problem.*

My mind raced. I lost track of why I was even at this big grand opening. Plans were taking form—a processing line for lobsters onboard a ship of some kind. As new ideas germinated and my focus became intense, previous projects slid to the back burner. This new endeavor required some deep thought. Festivities continued into the evening, and all had a great time at the exotic Atlantis Resort.

Then came the morning. Fun and games over. We all returned to our jobs in Seattle. My latest work included converting two Russian vessels that had arrived in Seattle, and another ship in Pusan, Korea. The new lobster catcher/processor project was relegating the two Russian conversions off to the slow part of my brain's activity. *No problem.*

I flew back to Nassau to get more details on what the financial investor wanted to do, and when. They would need a boat with a shallow draft and flat bottom. Next stop Savannah, Georgia, where a few potential boats were up for review. I found one that had been a Coast Guard buoy tender. The name on her stern was painted in big letters, *Goldenrod*. Not in great shape, she was nonetheless ideal, a 104-foot river tender with a flat bottom and shallow draft. She had room for crew quarters and a galley. The sale price wasn't too severe, though I thought a $140,000 was a little high.

Now the innovating process was to begin. I had to design the equipment to process a specific amount of lobsters per day. The lobsters had to be handled carefully so the long antennas remained intact. From the removal from the lobster trap to the processing system was a big deal for the marketing of whole cooked lobsters.

The packing of the lobster would entail insertion into a small mesh net, covering each lobster without breaking the antennas. Using my intrinsic innovating experience, plus a little imagination, I invented a device that would perform the task, drew up the design, and had Coastline make a stainless-steel sample unit. This unit was mounted near the cooling tank where the lobsters were being sorted for size. There an operator would put the lobster, tail-first, through the opening on the top of the unit. Then the netting was pulled up from the bottom, and the lobster was pushed down into the netting. The tail came out the bottom, and the operator grabbed tail and pulled it down with the netting around it, antenna and all. Voilà! You had a lob-

ster sealed in tight netting with antennas attached. And into the freezer it went.

All processing was done on the stern of the vessel. To make a survey and stability report and a blueprint with every detail drawn out required time at the drafting board. Because of the weight, the equipment for processing wouldn't fit in the space required. The test presented a bit of a problem. It became necessary to add a 10-foot section on the stern, to keep it above the water after all the processing equipment was secured and the tanks were full of water and product. We added the necessary extension, and the weight did not hinder the boat's stability.

Innovation inevitably meant mistakes made along the way. The first mistake was hiring the wrong guy to assist me, a local in the maritime business. He knew boats and had sailed on ships for the Department of Defense, and he had a tenderman's license—that said a lot about his knowledge of a ship's systems. He knew where to find just about anything I needed for the project. After a couple of months, however, his attention to detail faltered. He took it upon himself to move the *Goldenrod* to a shipyard and had them doing work I had not approved.

I was overloaded with working on the two Russian ships in Seattle undergoing conversions from fishing vessels to catcher/processors, as well as the boat project in Pusan.

I finally took a break and returned to Savannah. I had to remove the *Goldenrod* from the Savannah shipyard to Palmer Johnson shipyard in Thunderbolt, Georgia, down the river a few miles. This yard catered to multi-billionaires and their mega-yachts. We were not there very long, because the workers were slower than a sea slug crawling against the current, and each man-hour charge was exorbitant. Mistakes are not always realized until after the fact. I had to find a better yard. Atlantic Dry Dock in Jacksonville, Florida, proved to be the one to finish this project. They pulled her out and set her up on land where we could work together with the shipyard crew. (Most yards didn't allow the ship's crew to work on their boat themselves.)

We had not received any of the new equipment yet, and I was concerned I had made a terrible mistake just taking on this money-sucking project. There were also more problems with this old vessel than we were originally led to believe. A salesman will tell you anything to make a sale. We'd been assured the engines were operable and ready to run. After the sale was finalized, we discovered many things that were not as promised. In the end, it was my fault for not verifying claims and doing more thorough inspections. The engines were from Noah's ark and had to be replaced. We had to tow the *Goldenrod* to Jacksonville down the inland waterway. We insured it for a million. I prayed it would sink on the way there. No luck. They made it.

Meeting with the investors, I informed them what would be needed to finish. All work stopped, and I waited for a decision. Continue with the project, they told me. So I returned to Jacksonville. The yard required every detail to be illustrated to scale before they would touch it. Instead of just burning a hole through a bulkhead and sticking the pipe through it and welding in place, they required a scaled drawing of each detail before they would make a move. Once again, I spent a lot of time on my drafting board.

I got lucky when Jim Johnson joined me on this lobster conversion. Jim had a master's license and a chief engineer's license. The details for the processing of lobsters was catch, cook, sort for size, freeze, pack, and carefully store their netted bodies in the freezer hold.

The *Goldenrod* in drydock in Jacksonville, Florida, waiting to begin its conversion to a lobster-processing ship.

From the freezer they are packed in boxes. The freezer hold was forward, so I designed a tilt-up roller conveyor system that would accommodate the boxes of frozen product from aft to forward. The conveyor tilted up when traveling and down when fishing and processing. It worked perfectly!

The project finally completed, we lowered the vessel into the St. Johns River.

We still had a Bahamian crew on board, and we set sail for Andros Island to load lobster traps. Heading south towards Cuba, we set the traps. I went through every detail, walking the crew through the process. We were fitted out with completely new refrigeration compressors, main engines, generator, galley equipment, electronics, and 4,000 lobster traps. The crew was doing okay, but at times required a little motivation.

The vessel and her equipment functioned as designed without additional modification. My job was finished.

Jim stayed on awhile to keep the operation running smoothly. He could captain the boat, and if anything went wrong or didn't work, he could fix it. I felt an enormous gratification as an entrepreneur, idea guy, and inventor.

I left the Bahamas in a cloud of euphoria.

Licensed to Shell

Bahama lobster company looking for more
They want their lobsters in every store
They heard about catcher processors at sea
Word came about an innovative guy that creates
About any kind of designs for vessel remakes
Just what they were looking for to build it fast
Successful, completed, and built to last

24
Dynamic Design Changes

An exciting new beginning had reactivated my life. In an instant my brain was back to innovations, inventions, and ingenuity. An offer I couldn't refuse had entered my life. I needed this opportunity like I needed air to breathe.

We sailed my ship, the *Akutan*, from Alaska and tied up to the Seattle Trident Seafoods pier in the canal that separated Lake Union from Lake Washington. I had been gone for months processing Alaska King crab, and I was looking forward to being home with my family.

Jim Hilt, a friend and also a captain with several years in the Bering Sea, came aboard. He was employed by Marine Resources Company International (MRCI) located in Seattle. His boss had asked him if he knew of anyone with experience processing at sea. That's what brought him aboard the *Akutan*. Jim asked me if I wanted a change from being at sea for months at a time and if I would be interested in having a job that would allow me to go home every night? It required no more than a nanosecond to reply.

"What do you have in mind?" I asked.

"We're looking for someone with shipboard processing experience," explained Jim.

The offer grabbed my immediate attention, and I made an appointment with the president of MRCI. The company—half the owners were Russian—was in decline, because Americans were building their own factory trawlers to deliver to Russian motherships, and the need to repair and refit older Russian vessels was waning.

MRCI hired me, but I received no instructions or guidelines on just what I was supposed to do. I was shown to an office with a desk and a credenza with a little square box with a monitor and the logo of *an apple with a bite out of it*. I figured, as it was 1990, this thing must be a computer of some kind. That was my first problem. What am I supposed to do with this thing? Time moved along, and I had to ask, "How do you turn this thing on?"

Settling in, Tony Allison, MRCI president, asked me to go look at a system that a company was putting together for processing on board a ship. Jim and I scoped it out together.

"Whammo!" My brain circuitry kicked into warp speed, and I instantly had a vision. This was the kind of excitement I live for.

Somewhat stoical, I normally don't get too excited about much of anything, except when I get to see my wife, kids, and grandkids—*then I get excited*. But this creativity and innovation kind of excitement, it comes next!

I returned to the office trying to suppress my intense desire to blurt out my idea. I knew what would work on a vessel, but had no idea what kind of vessel was available for what I had in mind. It did not take too long before I found out.

While I enjoyed being home every evening, that pleasure did not last long. One week later, I was on a plane to Copenhagen, Denmark, then to Kristiansund, Norway. I toured a shipyard that was building a factory trawler. She was a beautiful ship, and I could picture myself at the helm. Next stop Oslo, Norway, then Stockholm, Sweden, then on to Helsinki, Finland, and finally Moscow.

In the Moscow offices of MRCI, we had a meeting that lasted for only one day, and then we flew across Asia to Vladivostok on Russia's eastern seaboard. We had scheduled meetings for several days all over far east Russia, working on convincing Russian companies to have MRCI manage their vessels, with some talk of possible vessel conversions.

Three weeks later, I was back in my Seattle office working on a layout for a processing line. Eight days after that I was back to Russia! This time I had the chance to go aboard a Russian fishing vessel classified as an ST503. I measured the deck space and logged it in my book. After more meetings, we finally convinced one company to let us convert their ST503 into a King crab catcher/processor.

Back in Seattle once again, my brain circuitry was blinding me to any other work. I went to my house and retrieved my drafting board and drafting machine. There wasn't enough space in my assigned office, so I was able to move to the biggest office on the corner of the building. I was able to set up all my equipment and enjoy a view of the canal.

Here is how it worked. I made some preliminary sketches, which gave me an idea just what will fit in the measured space on the vessel, that Russian ST503. Calculating what equipment and size would fit, I next went to Coastline Metal Fabricators in Bellingham, Washington. They offered some estimated costs for the equipment I needed. Then I hit them with the big one. Everything must fit in a container this size—and I show them the drawings. The container needed to be indestructible, made of aluminum, and weigh not over a specified amount, in order to maintain the stability of the ship in which it was to be secured.

I designed the cookers, cooling tanks, brine tanks, and glazing tank. The finished design and precise measured detail for manufacturing would be done by Coastline's draftsman, to determine how the product will be packed and what size each box of crab will be. I also needed to determine the height of the overhead in the container.

All dimensions secured, we knew what and how the tanks would be placed. Coastline accepted the project. I would still need to find a refrigeration compressor that would not only fit in the space but produce the necessary refrigerant to freeze the estimated product in the allotted time. My friend Lars Matthiesen of Sabroe Refrigeration had all the answers, and we made a deal to purchase the necessary equipment once the potential buyer accepts our proposal.

I then went on to design collapsible cooking baskets, and contracted Northwest Wire Company to manufacture them. Listing all the equipment, I discover I need more space to house the machinery away from the processing area, but still in the same container. I had forgotten the air compressor to operate the air hoist. *No problem.* There's room. The electric panel can be put in the machinery space.

I designed the container to fit up on the deck. The piping connections for water supply and electrical feed would come from the ship's systems. When the container was placed in the specific location on the deck of the ST503, all connections would fit without adjustments. In addition, this container could be removed and set up on shore and process there as well. Totally versatile! All that the unit would need was a water supply and electrical. Each corner of the container has been reinforced for the lifting eyes, making it totally mobile.

I contacted everyone and every company that had the necessary equipment to make everything come together, including prices and weights. At that point nothing had yet been purchased, but the vendors were ready to proceed. The shipyard owner and I spent hours in meetings with pencil and paper, until we agreed on the procedure and the price.

I presented the package to my boss, Tony Allison, for review and discussion. At first, he appeared to be a little skeptical, but I assured him we could make good money with this project. He asked how long it would take to do the conversion. I told him, after the equipment was completed for installation, we could finish in 45 days. The look I got was priceless!

We presented a proposal to a fishing company on Sakhalin Island, just north of Japan in the Sea of Okhotsk. They accepted our proposal. They brought their ship to Seattle, and the process began. A lot of work had to be done to the ship's deck and freezer hold, but it was completed in 45 days.

This is what makes me a happy man.

From that first refit, we went on to convert 31 more vessels. Not all of them in Seattle; some were in Pusan, Korea. Not ev-

GEAR

Russian
o
tyle

...nt relinquished control of the vessels, a new type of joint venture ...thed $15 million worth of life into the Seattle economy.

Before their conversion in Seattle, the 130' to 160' Russian trawlers had a tremendous amount of fishing equipment on deck: huge seine power blocks, big trawl winches, incinerator rooms, etc. Everything had to be taken off before turning them into modern crabber/processors. The Russians targeted crab, but did so in a relatively crew-intensive, inefficient manner.

Jerry Tilley, MRCI Director of Operations and Equipment Sales. "So, MRCI's general manager, Tony Allison, and others had several meetings with the different Russian kolkhozs and convinced them to harvest their own resource and sell a finished product, rather than sell off their quotas to foreign enterprises who would reap the profits."

Behind the Times

Although the Russians were already fishing crab, the fishery was underutilized and the product was inferior. "They usually fished with Japanese longline conical pots and cooked the catch in 1-ton cooking baskets," explains Tilley, "and their blast freezers were inadequate. It required 12 to 16 hours to freeze the crab, while brine freezing can do it in 30 minutes."

With a tentative agreement to convert the Russian vessels to American-style, pot-and-processing operations, Tilley came back to Seattle and began putting to-gether a consortium of American contractors with the required expertise. The Russians stipulated that all work had to be guaranteed 100%, and not everyone Tilley con-tacted was willing to do that. But the late Dave Tippett, former owner of Tippett Marine, was very enthusiastic.

"We drew a whole bunch of pictures," recalls Tilley. "You know how projects start out on napkins and paper towels, and we crunched a lot of numbers for a lot of days and weeks before we finally figured out what we could do it for. Then I went to the people at Sabroe, and they said they would guarantee everything 100%. Aurora Crane was willing to do it, too, so it is providing all the hydraulic systems equipment, power blocks and cranes. Coastline Equipment Co. in Bellingham is building the containerized processing equipment, and Harris Electric is doing the electrical work."

After putting all the parts and costs

JULY 1993 NATIONAL FISHERMAN 33

National Fisherman, an industry newspaper, featured Jerry Tilley in a 1993 article about the surge in converting Russian trawlers to crab processors.

ery container was for King crab. And not every vessel was identical. Each ship had different requirements for the container size and location of attachments. In the meantime, I also designed containers for salmon processing. Some of the ships sailed from Petropavlovsk-Kamchatskiy, Russia, to Dutch Harbor, which was only a three-day run. We installed one of the salmon containers there at Magone Marine.

The project kept me occupied, every refit functioned as planned, and every conversion was a truly satisfying experience. The intensity and demands of each project were what I loved about this job. I went again off to Russia for a 30-day adventure to look at more boats. I couldn't wait to feed my ideas—a little bit at a time—to company president Tony Allison.

Dynamic Design Changes

Marine Resources Company International
Needed someone to assist that was rational
An idea guy that could modify a ship's fate
Some change is good if it's not too late
Offer a design on a proposal with estimated cost
If they don't accept right now, all is lost
Except they did, everybody's happy all around
Soon we start because the ship is in Puget Sound

25
Tanner Queen Is Snow Surprise!

Fishing was good, and money was rolling in. The big problem many fishermen complained about was the flat-shelled skinny-legged crab that were invading their pots. The fishermen would throw these on the deck, stomp on them, then throw them overboard. Some areas were so thick with this Tanner crab pest, that fisherman would move to other areas where they could just catch King crab.

The Tanner crab caught around Kodiak Island were scientifically known as *Chionoecetes bairdi*. King crab fisherman had different names for them, names only a fisherman's vernacular could adequately describe.

Kodiak in the early 60s was a city on the way to becoming a thriving little fishing community and the number one fishing port in the United States for pounds delivered and value received. It would be known as the King crab capital of the world.

In those days the price of King crab was 8 cents per pound delivered to a tender, or 10 cents per pound delivered to a processing facility in the city. King crab fisherman worked on small boats, mostly 40–50 feet. Regulations allowed fishing with 30 pots. The pots were round, about 4 feet in diameter and 2 feet high. They fished for the King crab close to shore, and delivered their catch to the tenders that came into the bays near the fishing grounds. These tenders were mostly older sardine seiners that had been converted to live tank boats.

King crab in the early years around Kodiak averaged in weight about 12 pounds. Cooked sections (half a crab) average 4 pounds; a 10-pound box sold for $4.

The Tanner crab continued to plague the fishermen, so the fishermen soon developed modified gear that could catch King crab while allowing the Tanner crab to escape. Other crab fishermen moved to areas not previously fished and bought bigger boats and better gear that caught more King crab with less effort. The round pots were abandoned, and larger square pots became the norm. For the time being, Tanner crab was not a problem because it could escape from the newly developed pots.

Time marched on, and so did the King crab. Processing plants competed more and more, and prices went up accordingly. Fishermen looked for new areas, moving farther away from the islands and into open seas. Since processing was my expertise, as things changed in the crabbing industry, inspiration struck me. My creative mind set to work out new ideas about the Tanner crab.

Some of the smaller boats that were scratch fishing decided to bring in those flat-shelled, skinny-leg Tanner crabs hoping someone might figure out a way to process them for the market. I don't recall how many tried out the Tanner crab, but for about a year quite a few did. But they just couldn't get the meat out of the crab without generating a pile of shreds and shells. Selling frozen sections of an unknown species of crab was out of the question.

A new plant was built in Kodiak by the Japanese company Taiyo. The president of that venture was Bix Bonney, so they named the company B&B Fisheries. Bix Bonney hired me to oversee the construction and design of the processing systems for the production of King crab, Dungeness crab, salmon, shrimp, scallops, and halibut. When the King crab fishery was slowing down, and the plant had a lot of downtime, we had to come up with something to pay the bills. As production and processing superintendent, I had the idea I could develop a process to remove the meat from the Tanner crab in whole pieces rather than shreds, which were not a marketable product.

One of the fishermen in our fleet of boats brought us some of those unwanted skinny critters so I could experiment with them. After hours of trial and error—lots of error—I came up with a process that appeared to be successful, but still didn't produce more than 12% yield. Tanner crab have slender, elongated legs with a small opening where the leg connects to the body portion of the crab. This small opening didn't allow leg meat removal in one solid piece. However, cooking time and temperature was a key factor in the successful removal of the leg meat, especially the *merus*, which is the large portion of the crab leg.

Other processors had tried the same procedure used to remove the meat from King crab legs, that is, cooking the crab for 20–30 minutes and then feeding it into a set of rollers to extract the leg meat. The King crab leg shell opening, next to the body of the crab, is the same diameter as the merus, so by running it through a set of rollers, which looked like an old time washing machine wringer, the meat came out in one piece. But when they tried this procedure with Tanner crab legs, the meat came out in shreds along with large quantities of the shell.

Well aware that this process was not working, I realized that with Tanner crabs, the smaller shell opening of the crab leg had to be enlarged. By cutting the knob of the leg shell to the body at an angle with a band saw, then dropping each individual leg onto a moving belt through a cooking tank of water at 160 degrees for 9 minutes, the leg emerged from the water ready for the meat to be extracted. A worker would grab the leg and strike the shell on a padded edge of the tank; the merus would drop out in one piece! The merus then traveled on another belt through another cooking tank at 200 degrees for 12 minutes. After that, it dropped into yet another tank with a moving belt that cooled the product prior to being discharged onto a packing belt where it was packed into 5-pound blocks. The blocks were loaded on trays and frozen in a plate freezer at −35 degrees. The Tanner crab leg meat was so tasty coming out of the cooling tank onto the packing belt, that many of the workers were eating up the profits and lowering the yield considerably. We had to watch them constantly, and threaten them with no coffee breaks, no doughnuts, or immediate discharge. The direct discharge warning had no effect, but the promise of no coffee and doughnuts did the trick!

Eventually, all the problems were eliminated and success reigned. I was a very gratified individual. Never a doubt in my mind that I could find a way to extract the meat from this crab successfully. I almost broke my arm patting myself on the back.

We generated a small amount of the product and sent it off to some markets for consumer testing. For marketing purposes we called it *Chionoecetes bairdi*, "Queen" Crab. After several months we had a marketable product, and we started buying this newly developed crab species for 10 cents a pound. We only sold leg meat to start, and we sorted the crab so only the cleanest and most jumbo meat was shipped in sections. Eventually our Queen Crab became Snow Crab.

The *Kodiak Mirror* of April 17, 1968, headlined: "70,000 Pounds of Queen Crab Landed This Week." Here's a summary of the piece:

> Production of Queen Crab took dramatic upswing this week with the landing of approximately 70,000 pounds of live crab at B&B Fisheries by a number of boats. In addition, B&B Fisheries President Bix Bonney revealed that his firm is now proceeding with significant scale development of Queen Crab production. The firm has pioneered in the Queen Crab development during the past five months, taking increasing delivered of fishermen's catches.
>
> "We have full faith in the future of Queen Crab development and are now proceeding full speed ahead with this excellent seafood product," said Bonney. The firm is backing up their faith with a substantial investment in the New Queen product which has become a hot item in the seafood market, particularly on the East Coast where consumers claim it resembles their traditional Blue crab in taste qualities.
>
> The firm is processing both sections and meat on a large scale production now "and we are looking for more boats and a greater supply of Queen Crab," Bonney points out.
>
> "In the beginning we decided to experiment with this hitherto unused Queen Crab resource—it was sort of a fill-in item to provide our boats and cannery workers with additional hours of employment," said Bonney.
>
> "During the past five months we have shipped a number of van loads of Queen Crab sections and meat out as samples to various parts of the nation. We have been gratified at the immediate and excellent market reception of this gourmet item," he said.

Bonney attributes much of the success in production and handling methods to his top production expert, Superintendent Jerry Tilley.

"Initially we ran into the same production problems everyone else did—and many dropped the idea of trying to develop the Queen Crab resource because of the peculiar production problems encountered," said Bonney. "But Jerry Tilley persevered and finally prevailed, developing a production method that makes Queen Crab a feasible product. We call it the "Tilley Method," and he deserves recognition for making a real contribution to the development of what we believe will shortly become one of the largest major fisheries of the North Pacific," Bonney said.

"I cannot commend more highly the efforts of Jerry Tilley in his determination to make a success of Queen Crab production. He has proven to be an expert in the field of seafood production," Bonney said.

Years later, as bairdi (i.e., Tanner) crab production declined around Kodiak, fishermen found another Tanner crab in the Bering Sea, which was smaller in size but more abundant, the *Chionoecetes opilio*. This species became known as "opies." Hundreds and millions of pounds were caught, and the biggest buyers of the sections produced were the Japanese.

From there, the rest is history.

Tanner Queen Is Snow Surprise!

The deplorable little critters are plugging our pots
We get them aboard and stomp them, killing lots
King crab we are after, not crab no one wants to eat
How do we get rid of them or do we cry defeat
Take some to town maybe they will buy
Go to B&B where they have a pretty smart guy
He will know what can be done, it's not a mystery
He did just that, and the rest is history

Afterword

There is one crucial outlook that controls one's life. You are not born with it, but it affects you and those around you. As you mature, you develop an attitude—to be successful, make sure it's a positive one. Those who work around you, and those you work for, will notice. It is no accident. You are at the helm. Have no fear to try something new and different. Be creative.

Utilize that vacant space in your brain and activate the hidden potential that has remained dormant. Pay attention to your instincts. Make discouragement an opportunity to conquer any obstacle. That is when the vacant part of your brain sails into service. Use it. Never succumb to the pressure of the negative, as that will steer you into one sandbar after another. Chose a positive light that will guide you on a true course in life—captain your ship with a cargo full of positive.

Enter each day ready for the life that may require a fight
To change your mind to a positive attitude and keep in sight
Ignore any negative vibes, look forward to what you can do
Always think positive and forget any of your past review
If your mind is entering agitation and full of past strife
Remember that only you are the captain of your future life

Accomplishments

1943	Tilley Cannery: Canned crab; Westport, Washington.
1945	Tilley Cannery: Designed flow system to remove crab shell from meat; Westport, Washington.
1948	Tilley Cannery: Designed and built cannery in Blaine, Washington.
1952	Seattle Seafoods: Designed and built Dungeness crab plant and managed operation on Pier 60; processed halibut after crab season; Seattle, Washington.
1953	Ketchikan Cold Storage: Dungeness crab processing halibut; Ketchikan, Alaska.
1955	Northern Processors: Designed and installed equipment on first floating Dungeness crab processor in Alaska; done on a power scow.
1957–1960	Pacific Pearl Seafoods: Installed first shrimp peeling machine in Alaska; designed and built all equipment, processed crab, managed the plant; Wrangell, Alaska.
1958–present	Kodiak Elks: Member; initiated in Wrangell, Alaska, 1958.
1960	King Crab, Inc. (owned by Ocean Beauty): Managed plant, fixed machine problems, rebuilt all the canning machines, 100% increase in production of canned King crab; 10% increase recovery of shrimp line; redesigned salmon line; Kodiak, Alaska.
1961–1970	Aleutian Divers: Underwater commercial diver; installed underwater pipelines, made insurance underwater surveys, raised sunken vessels, performed underwater demolition, saved vessels from disaster; Kodiak, Alaska.
1962	Toastmasters: Member, Kodiak, Alaska.

1964 49th Star Seafoods: Designed and installed processing line for 8-machine shrimp peeling machine operation; Kodiak, Alaska.

1964 Shrimp fishing vessel *Fortress*, Kodiak, Alaska.

1964 –1970 Kodiak Volunteer Fire department: Founding member and president.

1964, 1966 Alaska two-time singles bowling champion.

1964–1970 Assistant Fire Chief: Kodiak, Alaska.

1965–1970 Fisheries Chamber of Commerce: Board member, Kodiak, Alaska.

1965–1967 Built King crab cannery processing plant on a barge, towed it to Kodiak, and managed it; Kodiak, Alaska.

1967 Alaska State Centennial Commission: Board member.

1967 Kodiak City Councilman.

1968–1970 B & B Fisheries, Kodiak, Alaska: Supervised the building of first plant; designed all equipment; developed the Tanner crab process.

1967–1968 Alaska King Crab Marketing and Quality Control Board: Chairman.

1968 King crab quality control committee: Chairman.

1968–1969 Created the first King crab quality control illustrated manual.

1968 Kodiak King Crab Festival: Event chairman.

1968–1969 Kodiak Navy League, President.

1969 JET Alaska Crab Processors: Processing and delivery; Kodiak, Alaska.

1970 Northern Processors: Operations Manager; rebuilt three operations and managed them, Kodiak, Alaska.

1971 Vita Foods: Operations Manager; redesigned and managed plant, built processing system on liberty ship; Dutch Harbor, Alaska.

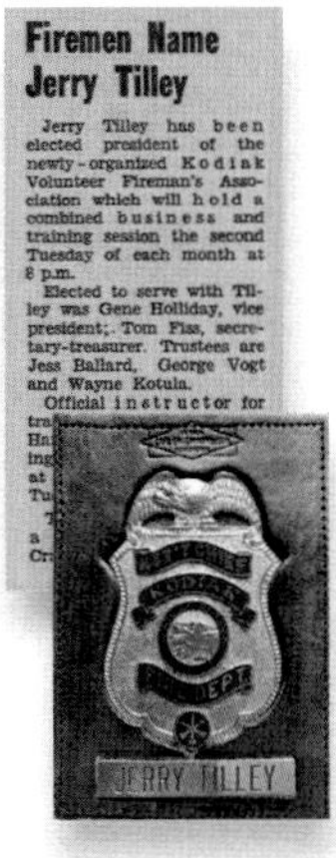
Firemen Name Jerry Tilley

Jerry Tilley has been elected president of the newly-organized Kodiak Volunteer Fireman's Association which will hold a combined business and training session the second Tuesday of each month at 8 p.m.

Elected to serve with Tilley was Gene Holliday, vice president; Tom Fiss, secretary-treasurer. Trustees are Jess Ballard, George Vogt and Wayne Kotula.

Official instructor for

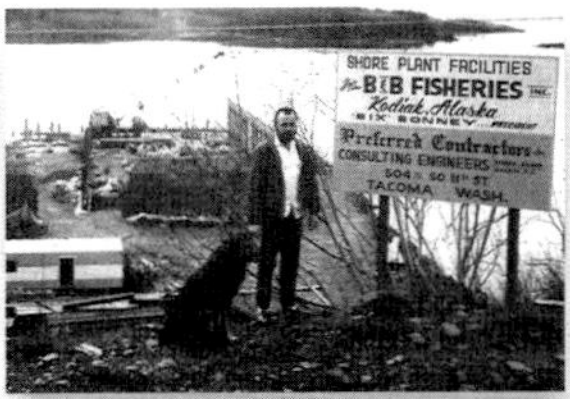

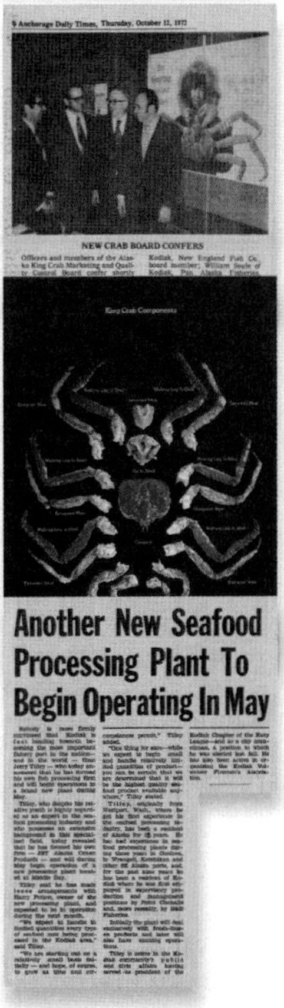
Anchorage Daily Times, Thursday, October 12, 1972

NEW CRAB BOARD CONFERS

Officers and members of the Alaska King Crab Marketing and Quality Control Board confer shortly ... Kodiak, New England Fish Co. board member; William Soule of Kodiak, Pan Alaska Fisheries

Another New Seafood Processing Plant To Begin Operating In May

1975–1982	SeaWest Industries: Vice President of Operations, Onboard Processing and Shore Base Processing; Edmonds, Washington.
1982	Chiriki River Fish Company, Panama: Operations consultant; rebuilt a shrimp and fish operation, including their shipyard.
1982	Palacios Fish Company, Quellon, Chile: Started a crab operation in Chile, putting 600 people to work, processing stone crab..
1982–1983	Rebuilt and activated crab plant in Punta Arenas, Chile.

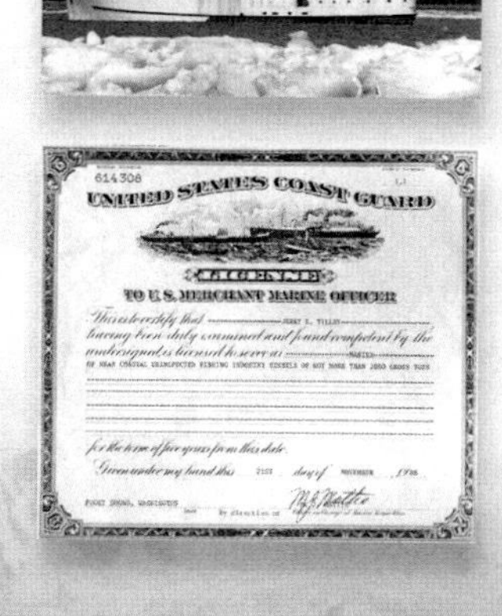
UNITED STATES COAST GUARD
LICENSE
TO U.S. MERCHANT MARINE OFFICER

1982–1990	Ship owner and captain of F/V *Akutan*: Bought, designed, and rebuilt the processing ship; processed crabs all over Alaska.
1986	Master's license: Earned 2000-ton master's license.
1990–1998	Marine Resources Company International (MRCI): Director of Operations and Equipment Sales; designed all equipment and supervised installation for 35 Russian fishing vessels, converted trawlers to King crab catcher/processors; Seattle, Washington; designed all equipment and converted a buoy tender to a lobster catcher/processor in Nassau, The Bahamas.

An Appreciation

I have known Jerry Tilley for a very long time and have admired him for what he has done and accomplished. This book is a fitting testament to his life and adventures. I want to take this final moment to express my heartfelt gratitude to Trudy Catterfeld of BookMarketingNext for the interest she took in this project, her knowledge of the book production process, and her grace and good spirit in making Jerry's *Ice & Fire* a reality!

Bob Simon
SunWave Properties, L.L.C.

Made in the USA
Monee, IL
04 October 2020